The
Jesus
Mystery

The Jesus Mystery

Of Lost Years and Unknown Travels

By Janet Bock

Aura Books
Los Angeles

Library of Congress Catalog Number: 80-67420

Published by Aura Books, A Division of Aura Enterprises, P.O. Box 46026, Los Angeles, CA 90046.

ISBN 0-937736-00-7

1st Printing Aug. 1980
2nd Printing Oct. 1981
3rd Printing May 1982
4th Printing Jan. 1983

TO MY FATHER

ERIK ALBERT WESTIN

1896 — 1962

For there is nothing hid, except to be
made manifest:
Nor is anything secret, except to
come to light.

Mark IV:22.

ACKNOWLEDGEMENTS

A number of people made important contributions to our film, "The Lost Years," and to this book.

From the moment the idea of a search for the missing years of Jesus occurred to him, my husband Dick was convinced of the importance of sharing it. His energy and determination kept it from being just another idea and made it a reality.

Our travels around India were to a large extent organized by our good friend Mr. Sohan Lal, who also took us into his home and in general provided the support systems necessary for such an ambitious undertaking. We also enjoyed the hospitality of Prasanthi Nilayam, the ashram of Bhagavan Sri Sathya Sai Baba, of the Ramakrishna Vedanta Center of Calcutta, the Sivananda Ashram of Rishikesh, and the Tibetan Community of Dharamsala. In Italy we were the grateful guests of Adrianna Monzeglio and her family, and of Mario Bianco during our visit to the Chapel of the Holy Shroud at Turin.

Our work was aided by Nick Cominos, Dr. Judith Tyberg, Mario Velez, Yaphet Kotto, Robert Dane and Ralph Graeber. I am particularly grateful to Larry Smith who generously contributed his spiritual sensitivity as well as his artistic ability to the realization of the painting for the cover, to Betty Geismer who typed the final version of the manuscript, to Sharon Chang whose contribution of time and energy has kept the office running in my absence, and to Linda Landes who recognized my initial hesitation and confidently encouraged me to "just plunge in."

My sincere love and appreciation go to the scholars and spiritual teachers who contributed their words and wisdom to this endeavor and, ultimately, to Bhagavan Sri Sathya Sai Baba . . . the source, the sustainer and the sustenance.

Janet Westin Bock
Hollywood, California
April 10, 1980

CONTENTS

Chapter I

WHAT 18 MISSING YEARS?

When my husband Dick first said to me, "Do you know there is a whole period in the life of Jesus that nobody knows anything about?" I thought he must be mistaken. How was that possible? Then, as I began to rummage through my memories of church and Sunday school, I felt a twinge of guilt, as though this was something very important I certainly must have been taught and then forgotten.

There were other memories of church though, of frantically trying to untie the handkerchief that had been knotted around a dime so it could be dropped in the collection plate, of Bible stories told with figures cut from colored velvet which stuck miraculously to the black cloth on the upright easel, of marching to "Onward Christian Soldiers."

Perhaps the clearest memory was of wanting to ask questions which were not answered in the stories, but being intimidated by fellow 8 year olds with memories for scriptural language and perfect attendance pins. I did have to admit, however, there was absolutely nothing in my mental storehouse that related to Jesus from the time he was 12 to the time he was 30. A quick check affirmed there was nothing in the Bible either. The second chapter of Luke, after telling of the incident in the temple when Jesus was 12 ends with the words, "And Jesus increased in wisdom and in

1

stature, and in favor with God and man." The next chapter begins with Jesus being baptized by John at what we are told is age 30.

Dick and I discussed the "lost years" over a period of months and gradually became engrossed in the subject. We felt it was important to us to try to find out what had happened during those years, years when an ordinary personality begins to take shape and is finally formed. And, more importantly, we felt our need to know, our yearning to fill the void was legitimate. This search was not a gauntlet thrown in the face of the Church. It was simply our way of attempting to resolve questions important to us.

We decided we needed to find information consistent with what is known and accepted about Jesus' life during the three years just before the crucifixion that are told of in the Bible. Those three brief years had changed the world forever. What message for humanity might the other 18 hold?

Our search for the lost years had been prompted by a book called the Aquarian Gospel of Jesus the Christ which we found contained information we had never seen before. With that as a catalyst, we began to look for other relevant material and soon heard of a book by a Russian, Nicolas Notovitch, who had traveled extensively in Afganistan, India and Tibet in the late 1880's.

Although his book was not readily available, we located a copy of the original 1890 edition. In it Notovitch tells a fascinating story of his travels which culminated in an accident (he was thrown from a donkey on a steep mountain path) that forced him to recover at a Buddhist gompa, or monastery, called Himis in Leh, Ledak, then the western region of Tibet and now the northern-most part of India.

In his travels Notovitch had heard enigmatic tales of a Saint from the west who had been revered by the Hindus and the Buddhists. While convalescing he was shown a copy of a manuscript, a collection of verses, describing the life of this Saint known as Issa, the Buddhist equivalent of the name of

2

Jesus. In the book "Caesar and Christ" Will Durant explains, "His parents gave him the quite common name of Yeshu'a (our Joshua), meaning 'the help of Yahveh': the Greeks made this into Iesous, the Romans into Iesus."[1] The story in the manuscript Notovitch was shown not only paralleled what the Bible says about Jesus, but included his life from age 12 to 30 as well.

Notovitch was told that the original manuscript was located in the great monastery on Mt. Marbour, near Lhasa, the capitol of Tibet, with other copies at several of the country's major monasteries.

Originally written in India and later brought to Tibet, the manuscript had been set down in the ancient Pali language shortly after merchant caravans brought news of Jesus' crucifixion. The copy shown Notovitch by the monks was in Tibetan and began, "The earth trembled and the heavens wept because of the great crime committed in the land of Israel. For there was tortured and murdered the great and just Issa, in whom was manifest the soul of the universe."

Notovitch's guide translated the verses which were written down and later reproduced in his book. Notovitch's belief in the authenticity of the manuscript was strong enough that he closed his introduction with the words, "I add that before criticizing my work, the learned societies could, without much expense, organize a scientific expedition, having for its mission the study of these manuscripts on the spot and thus verify their historical value."

Evidently no one accepted this invitation at the time because there is no record of anyone going to Himis to search for the manuscripts until 35 years later in 1922 when Swami Abhedananda went to Himis, saw the manuscript and wrote about it in his Bengali book of travels called "Kashmiri O Tibbetti." Unfortunately, since the Chinese takeover of Tibet and the reported destruction of monasteries, the hope of returning to search for the original, possibly of testing its age with modern carbon dating methods, is remote.

While reading the verses of what we came to think of as the Tibetan Legend, we were struck by their poetry and power, and by the uncanny similarity between this description of Jesus' life published in 1890, and the Aquarian Gospel, first published in 1911. We reached two possible explanations for the similarity. First, the Aquarian Gospel could be an amplification of the earlier Notovitch manuscript without giving credit to the source. Second, if the Tibetan legend is true, any subsequent telling of the story, whether by ancient manuscript or divine revelation, as the Aquarian Gospel was purported to be, would be basically the same.

Spurred on by each new piece of information, we began to look for corroborations of Notovitch's manuscript. We found information pro and con. The legend itself is difficult to defend or verify from a purely historical point of view as, we were surprised to find, is the Bible, and we would not have considered it as strongly had it not been for the validations from other fields. For example, discovery of the Dead Sea Scrolls which date from the same general period as the original manuscript, proved documents could survive the centuries.

Also, we came to be aware that over the years people who were accepted as psychics in a spiritual context, as well as spiritual leaders, had spoken of Jesus' missing years. Especially interesting were the remarks of Edgar Cayce who, in the course of his years as a trance medium, exhibited thousands of verifiable diagnoses and cures for people thousands of miles away. Cayce, an ardent, almost fanatical Baptist, was shocked upon first awaking from a trance to hear he had spoken of Jesus traveling and studying in foreign lands to the east. He later became convinced it was true.

It gradually dawned on us that those years were missing because someone had taken them out of the records, out of the Bible. We could not imagine Jesus would have appeared in Galilee at the age of 30 and hidden the major part of his life from the disciples he loved and asked to follow him. And it really doesn't seem possible those years were so unimportant as to be dismissed without a word.

So the idea grew that at some point what had been known about those years in his life had been deleted. In examining historical records of the early Christian church, it became evident that early church councils, especially the First Council of Nicea in 325 A.D. changed many points of doctrine, and it was possible those missing years were expunged because they did not coincide with the political needs of a growing church.

This then is what confronted our need to know, a need we have since found is shared by so many once the fact and potential significance of the missing years is grasped. As the bits and pieces of information began to fit together, we decided to make a documentary film, and by the time we were ready to begin, we had spent two years exploring the idea.

As I look back, it seems this outer search for Jesus was reflective of something going on within each of us. In our own way, we were working to clarify our spiritual understandings and to put them into practice. We were seeking forms of expression with lasting meaning, and this project filled that need. It seems that when we realized we would only be satisfied with directing our lives in search for truth in ourselves, were we then allowed and encouraged by coincidence or fate or God to search for the truth of Jesus' life.

An important factor, one we could not have known about when we began, was the series of lucky coincidences, the syncronicity which was to follow us on our journey and add immeasurably to both our personal experience and to the film.

Of course, the "truth" about the missing years in Jesus' life cannot be historically proven and, therefore, will always be subjective for each individual who explores it, which is the way it should be. We have no need to prove anything about this story. Rather, we share it with those who are searching, knowing they, too, will be guided.

Chapter II

THE LEGEND OF ST. ISSA

The prospect of following the path of Saint Issa was exciting. Directions in the legend were clear, place names could be traced, and the words of the long dead scribes who wrote down the reports carried a compelling sense of immediacy.

In writing about the legend, Notovitch said, "The two manuscripts, from which the lama of the monastery at Himis read to me all that had a bearing upon Jesus, are compilations from divers copies written in the Tibetan language, translations of scrolls belonging to the library of Lhasa and brought, about two hundred years after Christ, from India, Nepal, and Magadha, to a convent on Mount Marbour, near the city of Lhasa.

"These scrolls were written in Pali, which certain lamas study even now, so as to be able to translate it into Tibetan.

"The manuscripts relate to us, first of all, according to the accounts given by merchants arriving from Judea in the same year when the death of Jesus occurred, that a just man by the name of Issa, an Israelite, in spite of his being acquitted twice by the judges as being a man of God, was nevertheless put to death by the order of the Pagan Governor Pilate, who feared that he might take advantage of his great popularity to reestablish the kingdom of Israel and expel from the country its conquerors.

6

"One of the accounts, communicated by a merchant, refers to the origin of Jesus and his family, another tells of the expulsion of his partisans and the persecutions they had to suffer.

"Only at the end of the second volume is found the first categorical affirmation of the chronicler. He says there that Issa was a man blessed by God and the best of all."

The following is a condensed version of the legend published in 1890 by Nicolas Notovitch in his book entitled, "The Unknown Life of Jesus."*

I

1. The earth trembled and the heavens wept, because of the great crime committed in the land of Israel.

2. For there was tortured and murdered the great and just Issa, in whom was manifest the soul of the Universe:

3. Which had incarnated in a simple mortal to benefit men and destroy the evil spirit in them:

4. To lead back to peace, love and happiness, man, degraded by his sins, and recall him to the one and indivisible Creator whose mercy is infinite.

5. The merchants coming from Israel have given the following account of what has occurred:

IV

1. . . . the moment had come for the compassionate Judge to re-incarnate in human form:

---

*A complete transcript of the legend may be found in Appendix "A".

2. And the eternal Spirit, resting in a state of complete inaction and supreme bliss, awakened and separated from the eternal Being, for an undetermined period,

3. So that, in human form, He might teach man to identify himself with the Divinity and attain to eternal felicity:

4. And to show, by His example, how man can attain moral purity and free his soul from the domination of the physical senses, so that it may achieve the perfection necessary for it to enter the Kingdom of Heaven, which is immutable and where bliss eternal reigns.

5. Soon after, a marvelous child was born in the land of Israel. God himself spoke, through the mouth of this child, of the miseries of the body and the grandeur of the soul.

6. The parents of the infant were poor people, who belonged to a family noted for their great piety; who forgot the greatness of their ancestors in celebrating the name of the Creator and giving thanks to Him for the trials which He had sent upon them.

7. To reward them for adhering to the path of truth, God blessed the first-born of this family; chose him for His elect, and sent him to sustain the fallen and comfort the afflicted.

8. The divine child, to whom the name Issa was given, commenced in his tender years to talk of the only and indivisible God, exhorting the strayed souls to repent and purify themselves from the sins of which they had become guilty.

9. People came from all parts to hear him, and marvelled at the discourses which came from his

infantile mouth; and all Israel agreed that the Spirit of the Eternal dwelt in this child.

10. When Issa was thirteen years old, the age at which an Israelite is expected to marry,

11. The modest house of his industrious parents became a meeting-place of the rich and illustrious, who were anxious to have as a son-in-law the young Issa, who was already celebrated for the edifying discourses he made in the name of the All-Powerful.

12. Then Issa secretly absented himself from his father's house; left Jerusalem, and, in a train of merchants, journeyed toward the Sindh,

13. With the object of perfecting himself in the knowledge of the word of God and the study of the laws of the great Buddhas.

V

1. In his fourteenth year, young Issa, the Blessed One, came this side of the Sindh and settled among the Aryas, in the country beloved by God.

2. Fame spread the name of the marvellous youth along the northern Sindh, and when he came through the country of the five streams and Radjipoutan, the devotees of the god Djaine asked him to stay among them.

3. But he left the deluded worshippers of Djaine and went to Djagguernat, in the country of Orsis, where repose the mortal remains of Vyassa-Krishna, and where the white priests of Brahma welcomed him joyfully.

4. They taught him to read and to understand the Vedas, to cure physical ills by means of prayers, to teach and to expound the sacred Scriptures, to drive out evil desires from man and make him again in the likeness of God.

5. He spent six years in Djagguernat, in Radjagriha, in Benares, and in other holy cities. The common people loved Issa, for he lived in peace with the Vaisyas and the Sudras,* to whom he taught the Holy Scriptures.

6. But the Brahmins and the Kshatriyas told him that they were forbidden by the great Para-Brama to come near to those who were created from his belly and his feet;

10. But Issa, disregarding their words, remained with the Sudras, preaching against the Brahmins and the Kshatriyas.

11. He declaimed strongly against man's arrogating to himself the authority to deprive his fellow-beings of their human and spiritual rights. "Verily," he said, "God had made no difference between his children, who are all alike dear to Him."

16. "He alone has willed and created. He alone has existed from eternity, and His existence will be without end; there is no one like unto Him either in the heavens or on the earth,

17. "The Great Creator has divided His power with no other being; far less with inanimate objects, as you have been taught to believe, for He alone is omnipotent and all-sufficient.

18. "He willed, and the world was. By one divine thought, He reunited the waters and separated them

---

*The Vaisyas and Sudras are the lowest class of the caste system.

from the dry land of the globe. He is the cause of the mysterious life of man, into whom He has breathed part of His divine Being."

VI

1. *The white priests and the warriors, (Brahmins and Kshatriyas) who had learned of Issa's discourse to the Sudras, resolved upon his death, and sent their servants to find the young teacher and slay him.*

2. *But Issa, warned by the Sudras of his danger, left by night Djagguernat, gained the mountain, and settled in the country of the Gautamides, where the great Buddha Sakya-Muni came to the world, among a people who worshipped the only and sublime Brahma.*

3. *When the just Issa had acquired the Pali language, he applied himself to the study of the sacred scrolls of the Sutras.*

4. *After six years of study, Issa, whom the Buddha had elected to spread his holy word, could perfectly expound the sacred scrolls.*

5. *He then left Napaul and the Himalaya mountains, descended into the valley of Radjipoutan and directed his steps toward the West, everywhere preaching to the people the supreme perfection attainable by man;*

6. *And the good he must do to his fellow man, which is the sure means of speedy union with the eternal Spirit. "He who has recovered his primitive purity," said Issa, "shall die with his transgressions forgiven and have the right to contemplate the majesty of God."*

VII

1. The words of Issa spread among the Pagans, through whose country he passed, and the inhabitants abandoned their idols.

XI

1. Issa — whom the Creator had selected to recall to the worship of the true God, men sunk in sin — was twenty-nine years old when he arrived in the land of Israel.

Himis Monastery — where Nicolas Notovitch discovered the manuscript of the Life of Saint Issa.

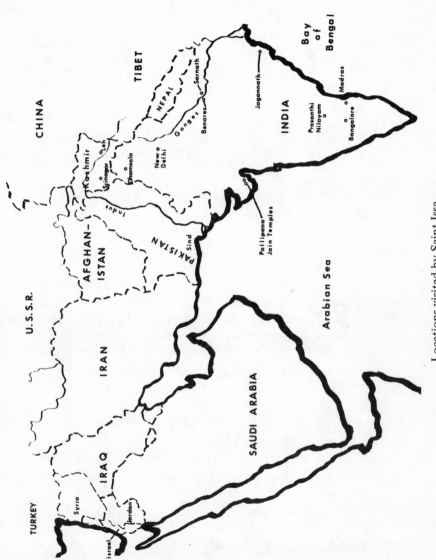

Locations visited by Saint Issa.

Chapter III

OUR JOURNEY BEGINS

The mind is a questioning thing. It wants to know and it wants to know why. So little is known of the actual life of Jesus from Biblical sources that the legend does not present contradictions to the Bible. Rather, it raises questions about the mysterious 18 missing years, the major part of Jesus' life, questions which have not been addressed, at least publicly, by church historians who have access to ancient records which still might exist. It would be best if we could each come to these questions with an unprejudiced mind, but that is hardly possible. So we bring along what we know, what we think we know, and whatever actual spiritual experience we may have had.

One of the first questions to arise in our minds was whether or not it had been possible to travel from Palestine to India 2,000 years ago. If it turned out to have been impossible the entire question of the validity of the legend would have been resolved immediately.

In the West we mark the beginning of modern time from the birth of Jesus and call it 1 A.D. However, to the Jews it was 3761 and to the Romans the year was 754. The Roman Empire extended to Great Britain and Germany in the north, Spain in the west, Ethiopia in the south, and the Arabian Sea and beyond in the east. All roads led to Rome. Caravans and ships traveled from the ends of the Empire, and Palestine was astride the natural trade routes between North Africa, Egypt, India and Rome. Travel could take months or years, but it was definitely possible. Even Saint Thomas, "doubting" Thomas, one of the chosen twelve, was to go to India after the death of his master and live out his life there.

With the first hurdle cleared, we came to the second. What would have made a young boy leave home and family to travel into the unknown?

The Bible tells of the incident in the temple when, after slipping away from his parents as they left Jerusalem following the Feast of Passover, the 12-year-old Jesus is quoted by Luke as saying to his worried mother, Mary, "How is it that you sought me? Know ye not that I must be about my Father's business."[1]

His Father's business had led the 12-year-old boy to stay alone in an unfamiliar city, far from home, for three days while he spoke with the elders in the temple, "both hearing them and asking them questions."[2] And, when his parents, to their great relief, finally found him, he appeared surprised at their concern, a concern that must have been heightened by the memory of circumstances surrounding his birth and the fact that Herod the Great had ordered the murder of all male children up to 2 years of age in an effort to kill this one child.

But what was going on in the mind of that 12-year-old who was hardly a child? What was the "business" that took his attention? And where, ultimately, did that searching spirit lead him?

The legend says:

> When Issa was thirteen years old, the age at which an Israelite is expected to marry, the modest house of his industrious parents became a meeting place of the rich and illustrious, who were anxious to have as son-in-law the young Issa, who was already celebrated for the edifying discourses he made in the name of the All-Powerful.

Then Issa secretly absented himself from his father's house; left Jerusalem, and, in a train of merchants, journeyed toward the Sindh,

With the object of perfecting himself in the knowledge of the word of God and the study of the laws of the great Buddhas.[3]

The Bible and the legend could easily be speaking of the same young man, adventuresome, intelligent and dedicated to the business of his heavenly Father.

And what of the religious thought that the young Jesus could have been exposed to in Palestine and Judea at that time?

In his book "Caesar and Christ," historian Will Durant says,

Sadducees, Pharisees, Essenes — were the chief religious sects of Judea in the generation before Christ. The most extreme of the Jewish sects was that of the Essenes. They derived their piety from the Chasidim, their name probably from the Chaldaic aschai (bather), their doctrine and practice from the stream of ascetic theory and regimen circulating through the world of the last century before Christ; possibly they were influenced by Brahmanic, Buddhist, Parsee, Pythagorean, and Cynic ideas that came to the crossroads of trade at Jerusalem.[4]

When the Dead Sea Scrolls were discovered in 1947, and identified as the work of the Essenes, it was hoped the ancient documents would provide new information and clear up some of the questions about the early Christian period. Dr. John C. Trevor, Director of the Dead Sea Scrolls Project at the Clairemont School of Theology in Southern California, was a student working in the Mid-East in 1947, and was the first western scholar to identify the writings and recognize their importance. Dr. Trevor has made the preservation and interpretation of the manuscripts his life work. When we called and told him of our interest and the film we were making, he agreed to talk with us.

Trevor said, "The discovery of the Dead Sea Scrolls, more than any other discovery we know, has enabled us, literally, to walk into Biblical history. The discovery shows that very period which spans the entire life of Jesus and yet, there is not a single reference to Jesus; there is not a single reference to any Christian point of view other than very vague relationships.

"Nevertheless, the scrolls shed a flood of light upon that very period of history that saw the birth, the early life and the teachings of Jesus.

"The orthodox position of the Christian church has been limited to the four gospel records as far as the early life of Jesus is concerned. Therefore, we have only the birth records and that brief account in Luke of the story at the age of 12. Thus, the church has continued through the centuries to assume that Jesus was in Galilee, probably in Nazareth with the carpenter family with which he was associated throughout those early years. And beyond that, very little has even been suggested.

"Now scholars even question the few traditions that appear in the gospels because they have earmarks of being theologizing of the church. Thus, the gospel of Mark, the earliest gospel, and the gospel of John lay the foundation for the average scholar's point of view of the beginning of the Christian story. In other words, the story of Jesus with John at the time of baptism is the beginning of the record as far as historical evidence shows us.

"One thing is historically clear, and that is that the earliest proclamation of the Gospel in the early Christian church was based upon the death, resurrection and the teaching of Jesus. Now speculations, of course, have been going on about the early life of Jesus and have put Jesus in many parts of the world, even including India."

So, with historical references which acknowledged the possibility of travel, as well as the influences of eastern thought, the idea of a young Jesus, eager to learn, leaving home for the east, entered the realm of the possible. In fact, he began to seem somewhat similar to so many young people in recent years who also traveled eastward on a spiritual quest.

We decided to retrace the legendary path of Issa and film what we saw. We wanted to visit the locations and observe the spiritual practices of the people. We wanted to find an indication of what Issa might have seen.

We had one definite advantage—air travel. Although by the end of our saga we had traveled by train, bus, car, rickshaw, pony and had breathlessly climbed mountain roads on foot carrying all of our camera equipment.

Our destination was India with a stopover in Rome en route. Because we were still on California time, that first day in Rome found us wide awake at 2:00 A.M., cameras ready, waiting for the sun to rise.

As we sat in silence on the steps of the Forum, watching the timid morning light etch the outline of the Coliseum against the sky, we seemed closer to ancient times. It was easy to feel the day unfolding as it might have one spring morning during the reign of Tiberius Caesar. We could imagine a courier bringing news of the provinces from Governor Pilate.

Was the crucifixion of a Jew mentioned in the dispatches? Did Imperial Rome recognize the seeds of the force that would prevail thousands of years after it had disappeared?

The Vatican is just a few miles from the Forum. To the visitor it is a representation in art of the awe and wonder of the Christian religion. But Jesus left no buildings or monuments. Rather, he left a lasting experience. And, for those who believe, he left teachings which enable us to realize that all people carry within them the potential of manifesting their own divinity.

18

In Matthew 13, verse 54, it is said of Jesus,

Where did this man get this wisdom and these mighty works? Is not this the carpenter's son? Is not his mother called Mary? Are not his brothers James and Joseph and Simon and Judas? And are not all his sisters with us? Where then did this man get all this?

Jesus replies, "A prophet is not without honor except in his own country and in his own house."[5]

"His own house," the place where the people knew his father, mother, brothers and sisters, but did not know where he had attained such wisdom.

The information in the legend seemed to say that Jesus' teachings were the culmination of his innate nature and intelligence as well as contact with other forms of thought, other religions.

If this is true, if the teachings of Jesus existed in other forms, we wanted to know.

Chapter IV

THE LEGEND IS VERIFIED

The most direct connection we found to the legend was the late Swami Abhedananda who in 1922 wrote that he saw the manuscripts from which Notovitch made his copies and subsequent translations. We knew Abhedananda had been a disciple of the famous saint Ramakrishna who was renowned in the late 19th Century for attaining union with God through the spiritual practices of all major religions, and he was a contemporary and brother monk of the well-known Swami Vivekananda.

Abhedananda was born in the 1860's, spent his early life in a monastery near Calcutta, and then traveled throughout India from 1888 to 1895. For twenty-five years, from 1896 to 1921, he lived in North America where he traveled extensively through the U.S., Canada, Alaska and Mexico. He made frequent trips to Europe to lecture and was acquainted with Thomas Edison, William James and Max Mueller, among others.

Swami Abhedananda was fascinated by Jesus as a spiritual personage so after reading Notovitch's book his curiosity was aroused and he decided to make the journey to Himis to see for himself. His visit takes on added importance because he was skeptical of Notovitch's claim and his objective in making the long, arduous trek was to expose Notovitch. Also, he spoke the language and could communicate more easily and directly than the Russian. When he found that the ancient writings did exist he wrote about them in his Bengali book of travels entitled "Kashmiri O Tibetti."

His disciple, Swami Prajnananda, is a musical scholar and author as well as the current head of the Ramakrishna Vedanta Math of Calcutta, a monastery and school which was founded by Abhedananda in the late 1920's.

Our plane touched down at Calcutta's Dum Dum Airport and soon we were in a taxi crawling through the maze of streets filled with traffic—four footed, two footed and motorized, of all descriptions. We had written ahead to introduce ourselves and our purpose so when we arrived we were greeted by Swami Prajnananda with tea and fruit in his book filled study.

Then, after showing us the shrine to the memory of his beloved guru, he settled back and invited us to switch on our tape recorder and begin our questions.

Dick:
    Swami, would you tell us about the visit of your guru, Swami Abhedananda, to the Himis monastery in Ladak?

Swami Prajnananda:
    Yes. After 25 years in America he returned to India in 1922. He read Notovitch's book and became very interested in the subject. He wanted to know if the scrolls existed and if Notovitch could have seen them. He went to Tibet in 1922 and he found the scrolls and he translated all the writings, all the life incidents of the Christ. He narrated those incidents in his book "Kashmiri O Tibetti."

Dick:
    What has happened to the manuscripts since Swami Abhedananda saw them?

21

Swami Prajnananda:

He went there and I have heard from his own lips that he saw the scrolls and he translated from them. Years afterwards he inquired but they said the scrolls were no longer there. I also requested to see the scrolls, but there is nothing. There are no scrolls. They have been removed, by whom we do not know.

Dick:

Apparently there were other copies that existed in other Tibetan monasteries.

Swami Prajnananda:

Yes, Swami has written in his book that the original manuscript was in Pali (an ancient language of the Himalayan regions). The Pali manuscript was originally in the Marbour Monastery. Do you know the Marbour Monastery?

Dick:

No.

Swami Prajnananda:

At the Marbour Monastery there was the original copy which had been written in Pali. But now there is no trace of it.*

Dick:

Are you interested in Christ?

Swami Prajnananda:

Yes. I am very interested in Christ. My guru used to say He, Christ, was an Indian yogi. He wrote a

---

*The Marbour Monastery was in Lhasa, the capitol of Tibet. Since the invasion of Tibet by China in 1947 the fate of Tibetan monasteries and their contents is unknown.

book called "Was Christ a Yogi." In that book he told that Christ was more than a yogi, that He practiced yoga and also that He realized God as not only Christian, but Hindu, Jain, Buddhist and the God of all faiths.

Visitors to the remote monasteries of Ladak, particularly Himis Gompa, seem to have been few and far between; however, another such traveler was the Russian artist Professor Nicholas Roerich who also reported hearing stories about the manuscripts during a brief visit to the monastery about 1925. Roerich's account was published in the west and comparisons were made with Notovitch's book, printed 35 years before. Those who could not or would not consider Notovitch's account dismissed Roerich as well.

Apart from the fact that Ladak was closed to outsiders until 1974, it is one of the most difficult places in the world to approach. In the months when travel is possible, the landscape is rocky, desolate and barren. The approach from eastern Kashmir is over a narrow mountainous track, barely suitable for army jeeps and frequently wiped out by landslides. The extremely high altitude, over 14,500 feet, makes necessary a period of gradual adjustment to the low level of oxygen before normal physical activity can be resumed.

The present Himis Gompa is over 400 years old. The writings it houses came from its parent monastery, Go San Gompa, which stood for well over 1,000 years before it deteriorated to the point it had to be replaced by the newer structure. Visitors to Himis have testified to the fact that its inner rooms are filled to the rafters with stacks and bundles of uncataloged writings which have accumulated over the centuries.

A recent visitor to Himis was Robert Ravicz, Ph.D., professor of Anthropology at California State University at Northridge. Ravicz had a special interest in Tibetan culture and, since Ladak was part of Tibet prior to its present status as a territory of India, and its culture is still Tibetan, he was eager to make the trip.

While at Himis in 1975 Ravicz learned of the legend. In a discussion with the Head Abbot, he was told that the texts and documents in the monastery could be studied by people coming from abroad, but it would take great effort and would be an arduous task. According to Ravicz, the research possibilities are there. He was told it would be necessary for someone to live in the monastery for several years and learn classical Tibetan before being allowed to look into the materials. Ravicz concluded a scholar would have to be highly motivated and really committed to the research possibilities.

This was as far as we could go to validate the existence of the legend. We knew it had been seen and written about by Notovitch in 1886 and 36 years later by Swami Abhedananda. We knew also that scholars with time and determination might be allowed to search again the musty chambers and unlit corridors of the sprawling 400 year old monastery once the lamas were convinced of their ability and sincerity.

We had good reason to believe the manuscripts had existed, and had been seen and translated. Now it was the path of the legend itself we were to follow.

Swami Prajnananda (left) and Richard Bock (right)
at the Ramakrishna Vedanta Math, Calcutta.

Chapter V

YOUNG ISSA DEPARTS

Our eyes may well be the windows of the soul, they are also the lenses looking outward which, when turned by the mind, bring into focus the world around us. A mind focused on itself struggles endlessly to bring nature to its knees in surrender. A mind focused inwardly on God is nurtured, supported and fulfilled by the very creation it no longer needs to control.

But what did the eyes of a 13 year old see, and what did his mind make of it all?

Jesus was born en route to Bethlehem. He escaped into Egypt with parents who left behind home and family to guarantee his safety. The Lord provided for their needs, security came from Him, not from externals. So it was that the seeds of a wandering nature would have been planted early, growing in 13 years to a fearless desire to discover what lay beyond the distant hills, beyond the teachings of the temple.

Then Issa secretly absented himself from his house; left Jerusalem, and in a train of merchants, journeyed toward the Sindh, with the object of perfecting himself in the knowledge of the word of God and the study of the laws of the great Buddhas."[1]

Desert caravans depart before dawn in the hour when the air changes from night to day, before even the quickening light reveals the mist rising from the ground. Morning sunlight provides the spectacle of color teasing night from the depths of indigo to sapphire, then chases it from the sky altogether before an advancing cavalry of gold, saffron and scarlet. The night tries to linger in purple shadows behind dunes and rocks, but there is no escape.

A boy of thirteen, wise for his age yet still a boy, eager to be off before it was discovered he had left his bed, would probably have been more interested in the animals than the beauty of the sunrise. Horses snorting and stamping, raising dust that would follow them into the heat of the day. Camels rising in jerky stages, shifting weight from bony knees to huge padded feet, ready to carry their burdens of oil, grain and fish from the farmers and fishermen of Galilee. Mules and donkeys giving one last defiant bray before unplanting their hooves and starting forward.

Perhaps Issa was leading one of the smaller donkeys, talking to it and urging it on as the morning sun stepped higher, intensifying warmth into heat. His own body protected by robes, his head covered with cloth bound with rope contrasted with the animals as they foamed and sweated, a stench rising from them in hot shimmering waves. The only respite the next oasis or caravansary where there would be water, shade and food.

Progress is literally step by deliberate step whether through Saudi Arabian deserts with unending dunes and heat, or over high plateaus and valleys surrounded by the mountain forests of Iraq and Iran. The wilderness is uninhabited by men, but populated with jackals, wolves, hyenas, deer, lions and tigers which screech and scream at passing parades of intruders.

Issa's destination was first the Sindh, where the Indus River fans out into myriad tributaries to create low-lying plains, deserts and swamps along the shores of the Arabian

Sea between Pakistan and India. Then he was to cross Northern India to the area of Orissa where the great temple of Jagannath stood, as it does today, at the center of Hindu learning and tradition.

The legend indicates Issa left his father's house at the age of 13 and arrived "this side of the Sindh" in his 14th year. A year, perhaps more, of travel, learning to survive as a man, and all the time wondering if the questions which prompted him to leave home and filled his mind much as the stars filled the night time sky of the desert would be answered once he arrived.

The legend says:

> *Fame spread the name of the marvellous youth along the northern Sindh, and when he came through the country of the five streams and Radjipoutan, the devotees of the god Djaine asked him to stay among them.*[2]

When the travels of young Issa brought him into contact with the Jains, their customs and practices were already over 500 years old. Jainism had been founded by a young man of wealth and noble birth named Varadhamana. Although his father was a chieftain of a powerful family, Varadhamana abandoned his position to become a wandering mendicant who practiced severe austerities, eventually walking through the countryside "clad only in the sky."

This period in the earth's history, the 6th Century B.C., saw tremendous intellectual and philosophical activity which, amazingly, has remained potent up to the present. In Israel the prophet Jeremiah was expounding the importance of moral character over ritual and sacrifice, in China Confucius was teaching a code of behavior comparable to the Golden Rule of the Bible, in Persia Zarathustra taught that the choice for humanity was between truth and evil, in Greece philosophers debated whether or not all life arose from a single source, and in India Varadhamana was to found Jainism even as the saga of Prince Gautama Buddha was beginning.

Varadhamana accepted the basic Hindu doctrines of his time but emphasized that the purpose of life was to purify the soul. Such purification was hindered by actions such as lying, stealing, and especially by harming any living thing. While none of Varadhamana's writings have survived, the Jain form of the Golden Rule, dating from the 4th Century B.C. has endured.

> Thus we enjoin on you, thus do we say,
> Thus we believe, thus we proclaim to all:
> No living things should be slain anywhere,
> Nor ordered forcibly this way or that,
> Nor put in bonds, nor tortured any way,
> Or treated violently otherwise;
> Because you are that same which ye would slay,
> Or order here and there against his will,
> Or put in prison, or subject to pain,
> Or treat with violence; ye are that same;
> The Self-same Life doth circulate in all.[3]

Before leaving for India we had the good fortune to meet His Holiness Muni Shshil Kumarji, a monk and leader of the Jain faith. When we met Muniji, the "ji" is added as a term of endearment, he was wearing a gauze mask over his mouth and nose to avoid the possibility of breathing in and harming anything alive in the air. He also carried a broom with soft cotton tassels with which to gently sweep the path before him as he walked so he would not harm any living creature.

Muniji spoke no English but used an interpreter. At our first meeting we sat in an audience of 200 to listen to him speak. The following day when talking to a friend who had also been there, hearing myself comment on the joy of his nature and the warmth of his smile, I suddenly had to stop and laugh. Here I was, extolling the warmth of a smile I had never seen. Muniji, in spite of the mask, or perhaps because of it and the love for life it represented, had affected us all with the sweetness of his nature.

In our subsequent meeting, Muniji explained briefly what the Jains believe about the possibility that Jesus was in India.

> We believe that Lord Jesus Christ did come to India at a place called Pallipana in the Guggerat district* where there is a big Jain temple, and he came into contact with Jain monks whose main precepts are non-violence, peace and love. We believe Jesus Christ did a lot of austerities there alongside Jain monks. He accepted the vows of the Jain monks about celibacy, about non-violence, about vegetarianism, about doing good to the common people; and we still have a lot of commonality between Jesus Christ's teaching and the Jain sect.

The most significant difference between these Jain precepts and those of Judaism in Issa's time can be found recounted again and again in the Bible, both Old Testament and New. One example occurred after the Lord revealed the commandments and laws of the covenant with Israel. Moses built an altar surrounded by 12 pillars, representing the sons of Jacob and the 12 tribes of Israel,

> And he sent young men of the people of Israel, who offered burnt offerings and sacrificed peace offerings of oxen to the Lord. And Moses took half of the blood and put it in basins, and half of the blood he threw against the altar.

---

*Pallipana is located in the Sindh area of Western India, south-east of the Indus River in Gujerat State. Its location corresponds precisely with the path of Issa described in the legend.

Then Moses took the blood and threw it on the people saying,

> Behold the blood of the covenant which the Lord has made with you.[4]

Sacrifice was the Israelites' way of relating to God at times of thanksgiving, danger, harvest, or planting. Later temples had permanent altars for sacrifice. Sacrifices were also prescribed to celebrate the birth of male children, and so one was carried out shortly after Jesus' birth.

> And when the time came for their purification according to the law of Moses, they brought him up to Jerusalem to present him to the Lord . . . and to offer a sacrifice according to what is said in the law of the Lord "a pair of turtledoves, or two young pigeons."[5]

The practices of sacrificing animals in an attempt to appease, cajole or please the Lord were part of the ritual worship Issa saw every day while growing up. They could not have been more different from the Jain belief that all life was sacred, divine, as much a part of God as each human being.

Through the Jains, Issa was presented with a teaching which said it was not animals that needed sacrificing, rather it was the mindless, animal-like qualities in men and women which needed to be purified, made sacred and finally surrendered.

At most the sacrifice of an animal represented the money necessary to buy it, but what greater wealth of awareness, discipline and self-control could be developed in attempting to overcome brutish tendencies and appetites. This encounter with the Jains was Issa's first concrete experience of another faith, another way of perceiving God.

The non-violent, ascetic nature of the Jains is reflected in

the caves of Khandagiri south of Calcutta in the State of
Orissa. Carved out of a granite hillside about 100 B.C. and
located barely four miles from the great temple of Jagannath,
Issa's second destination, the caves exist, apparently unchanged since Issa's time.

We had heard of them quite accidentally and so climbed
the time-worn stones to reach them with eagerness. Half way
up the steps a magical moment occurred. From a small
cluster of mud and thatch huts just to the right of our path
stepped a bearded, half-naked sadhu (renunciate) who
turned, examined us slowly with deepset black eyes, and
silently disappeared up the hill into the caves, leaving behind
a timeless impression that seemed to connect us with the
solitary figures of the past who had also climbed these steps.

What had been only shapes and outlines from the bottom
of the hill became carvings of animals and tall human figures
as we neared the top. We paused to read the sign,

> The twin hills of Udayagiri and Khandagiri con-
> tain excavated caves utilized for Jain monastic re-
> treats, datable from 100 B.C. to the early years of the
> Christian era.

The caves face south and east toward Jagannath, which
can be seen looming in the distance. The caves to the east
form a semi-circle around a secluded field where animals
roam and graze. They were cut from the rock to form
cubicles along a connecting verandah which is open on one
side and studded with carved pillars against which larger-than-
life human figures recline. The four-foot high space between
the top of the doorways and the ceiling of the verandah was
also covered with carved figures depicting harvest scenes.

While animals grazed below, we climbed inside. The caves
were silent with the stillness that resounds in great cathedrals,
or any place which has been a vortex of devotion and
spiritual practices through time. If the legend has a basis in

fact, if what the Jains of India believe is true, and if Issa did spend six years at Jagannath, which was now clearly visible in the distance, it is very possible he visited these caves and touched these very stones.

The Jain Caves of Udayagiri and Khandagiri, dating from from 100 B.C.

Chapter VI

LORD OF THE UNIVERSE

The legend says:

But he left the worshippers of Djaine and went to Djagguernat, in the country of Orsis, where repose the mortal remains of Vyassa-Krishna, and where the white priests of Brahma welcomed him joyfully. [1]

Jagan-nath means Lord of the Universe and the mammoth temple of Jagannath at Puri where the legend says Issa lived for six years is one of the major shrines of Hinduism. It is often difficult for people in the West to get beyond the concept that Hinduism worships many gods, is polytheistic, when in fact it acknowledges one God who is boundless in attributes and manifestations.

Here Issa would have been taught that everything in creation is God's manifestation. The ancient scriptures of Vedanta, the philosophy behind the many and varied religious practices we lump together and call Hinduism, says the world was created when God uttered the primordial sound of "OM." The Bible says, "In the beginning was the word."

What may appear to us as polytheism is actually people worshipping the aspect of God to which they feel closest. Just as each of us may be someone's child, someone else's

33

spouse, brother or sister, employer or friend, but not six different people, so the fact that God is perceived as the embodiment of righteousness in one manifestation, as the overcomer of obstacles in another, and as the source of learning, strength or wealth in still others, means that the one God is all pervading. It does not mean each is a separate God mutually exclusive of all the others.

Over the ages sects have developed in India which forgot or ignored it, but this fact prevails at the basis of the scriptures and from time to time great teachers come to restore this truth to common currency.

One such teacher, if we believe the legend, was Issa. The Issa of the legend and the Jesus of the Bible were both committed to restoring the truth of ancient scriptures, to exposing the vested interests of priests and to restoring a direct and unhindered relationship between the individual and God.

The legend says,

> *Issa lived in peace with the Vaishyas and Shudras,*
> *to whom he taught the holy scripture.* [12]

The Vaishas and Shudras were the lower castes in a system which, when Issa found it, had degenerated from a concept originally stated in the scriptures as designed to support the orderly functioning of society. In this system various tasks necessary to the smooth running of the community were assigned to individuals and were equated with parts of the body of God. Some jobs were done by the head, others by the hands, still others by the stomach, legs, feet, etc. Each person who carried out a job represented a part of the body of God, everyone was equally a part of God.

The system acknowledged the different functions, but gave those who performed them equal standing. The jobs were different, the people equal. Then, someone decided his own function was superior to another's, that he was superior to another, and so the degeneration began. The human race has yet to experience a time when all people are valued for their innate divine nature, the one trait we share, rather than the qualities which differentiate and separate us.

The approach to the temple of Jagannath is along a broad avenue where a quarter of a million people gather each summer as they have since before the time of Issa, to view the procession of the three principal deities, Jagannath, his brother Balabhadra and Subhadra, their sister. Tradition says that a king wanted to behold the image of God as Lord of the Universe. God told him a log would be found in the sea with special markings and that the image of the Lord could be carved from this log.

When no mortal carpenter could even chip the log, the Lord descended in the form of an old man who offered to carve the image on the condition he be left undisturbed in a closed room for 21 days. After 10 days when no sound was heard from behind the door, the King broke his pledge and opened the door. He found three unfinished carvings—Jagannath and his brother were carved from the waist up with only stumps for arms, and Subhadra had no arms at all. The distraught King built a temple and conveyed the images there in imposing chariots.

Now, every summer the images are taken from the temple to a garden house called Gundicha Ghar about one mile from the temple. Three enormous chariots are constructed and decorated with a replica of the Jagannath dome. These four-story high chariots rest on huge wheels which are pulled through the immense crowds by pilgrims hoping to be blessed by the deity and freed from the cycle of birth and death.

As we approached the temple in late September the streets were almost empty. We learned that only certain castes of Hindus were allowed in the temple and since we were outcasts we would not be able to enter. One solution proposed by our taxi driver would allow us to see it anyway. The plan was to take us to the roofs of the buildings surrounding the temple walls. This would allow us to see inside and photograph with our telephoto lenses. The first building we tried was just across from the entrance and, after a suitable bribe had been paid because it was a municipal building which was closed that day, we clambered up a series of steps and ladders to reach the roof. From that vantage we could see the rectangular shape of the compound.

The temple stands on elevated ground surrounded by two walls with a gate on each of the four sides. The main gate, facing east, is called the Lion's Gate.

Inside the walls are shrines ranging from niches in the walls to large temples. The main temple has four inter-connected chambers—the hall of offerings, the dance hall, the assembly hall and the inner sanctum at the base of the towering dome which can be seen for miles around. It is here the wooden images of Jagannath, his brother and sister dwell and are worshipped daily by the faithful.

Our next vantage point was the roof of a building on the opposite side of the grounds. After a hurried conversation with someone in the house, we were led up a spiral path. The house was built around a small open shaft so we would climb one flight of stairs and then walk through the living quarters of the family on that floor to reach the stairway to the next level. The ascent to the roof was like going through layers of an archeological dig, each layer revealing details about the lives of its inhabitants.

From this roof we could see into the inner courtyards of the compound, and the entrance to a very vital part of the temple, the kitchens. We learned there are 1,500 hereditary attendants ranging from cooks and carpenters, potters, painters and other artisans, to priests, decorators and an official keeper of the seal. The immediate attendants are divided into 36 categories. The cooks are among the most important. Elaborate menus are prepared daily for the deities and their human followers. On festival days a meal might consist of 39 courses.

In the flat-roofed temple kitchens food is cooked in a hygienic fashion in a process resembling steam cooking. Many varieties of rice, curries, savouries and sweets are prepared every day. The cooks wear a cloth mask covering the nose and mouth. The kitchens are probably among the largest in the world as they cater to more than 10,000 people daily. There is a tradition here which dictates that all castes partake of food from the same plate. This rule was laid down by Mahalakshmi, the consort of Jagannath.

The real drama of Jagannath was the one going on just outside the walls, cast with the ill, the elderly, the devastatingly poor and the lepers whose truncated limbs mirrored the unfinished arms of Jagannath. They, as we, were outcasts and could not enter, but they live on the ragged edges of a struggling society supported only by the philanthropy of tourists who might fling them a coin just so they would go away and leave them alone.

I first encountered such poverty in the Orient when I was part of a group of college exchange students. I remember feeling smug because I lived in a country where there were, I thought, no beggars. Later, when returning from two years in Europe I was in Amsterdam and was astonished to see transients sleeping in doorways. Then, on my return to New York I passed through the Bowery. I lost my smugness.

Poverty and disease seem to be part of the human condition. When Buddha saw the sick, poor and dying he renounced his heritage as a prince and sought enlightenment. Now when I see beggars I try to deal with the feelings that surge up inside. Those reactions usually serve as a barometer of my emotional condition. If I am feeling insecure, my mind can reject their existence completely. If I am feeling tired the thought of them weighs me down further. If I am feeling guilty the sight can magnify my sense of guilt.

There is only one philosophy I have found that helps me understand the seeming inequality that abounds in the world, an idea which is fundamental to several schools of thought.

I heard it first in Sunday school, "Do unto others as you would have others do unto you," usually spoken in hushed tones of reverence. This Golden Rule seemed to be good public relations, and good for telling others how to behave, but it did not seem to be taken seriously by those who proclaimed it the loudest.

The next version was in high school physics and was presented as Newton's Law which states "for every action there is an equal and opposite reaction." This seemed to work, but it was limited by man's ability to measure and perceive. It didn't take into consideration anything beyond our present, limited knowledge. This might be OK for science, but was it enough when the major experiences of life, thoughts and feelings were excluded?

The third time I heard it something clicked. It made sense, and it made sense of everything else, at least for me. This time it was the Philosophy of Action, of Karma. It said the Golden Rule was right and Newton was right . . . we should do unto others as we would have them do unto us because . . . for every act we commit there is an equal act returning to us. Putting the two together was a subtle threat, giving each of us the responsibility for ourselves. We are, then, at the mercy of the inevitable rebound of our own actions.

But what about the beggars on the doorstep of the Lord of the Universe?

I read the words of Swami Vivekananda which say,

> Helping others physically, by removing their physical needs, is indeed great; but the help is greater according as the need is greater and the help more far-reaching. If a man's wants can be removed for an hour, it is helping him indeed; if his wants can be removed for a year, it will be rendering him more help, but if his wants can be removed forever, it is surely the greatest help that can be given him.

Spiritual knowledge is the only thing that can destroy our miseries forever; any other knowledge removes wants only for a time.[3]

This is the knowledge we were looking for. Did Issa find it when he studied here, was he forced to confront himself, as we were, by this place?

Jagannath is the pebble someone skipped along the surface of my lake. All may again appear quiet, but the stone sank to the bottom and ripples are running below.

Towers of the Temple of Jagannath.

A temple Interior at Jagannath.

Chapter VII

THE RIVER OF LIFE AND DEATH

The legend says:

> *He spent six years in Jagannath, Rajagriha,*
> *Benares and other holy cities.*[1]

At the time of Saint Issa, Benares was flourishing as the holy city of Hindu learning. The greatest scholars lived and taught there. By chance we arrived in Benares on Ram Leela, its most important holiday.

The Ramayana by the sage Valmiki is the oldest of the Sanskrit epics. Western scholars date it from at least 500 B.C., while Indians date it from the aeons long before it took written form. It is the dramatic story of Lord Rama, an Avatar.

According to the scriptures, all human beings are proceeding along an evolutionary path which will eventually culminate in the goal of mergence with God. As such, some are further along than others. An Avatar, on the other hand, is the descent of divinity into a human form for the specific purpose of helping others to achieve the goal by his guidance and example.

An Avatar is recognized by his actions. He has control over the five functions of the body (speaking, eating, reproduction, elimination and motion), control over the five senses (taste, touch, smell, sight and hearing), and control over the five elements of nature (earth, air, fire, water and ether). In addition to these fifteen qualities called kalas, all of which can be attained by humans through spiritual disciplines and practices, an Avatar has a sixteenth quality not attainable by humans, the quality of omniscience. Because his consciousness is unconfined by desires of a human body or of nature around him, an Avatar lives as an extension of divine purpose.

Needless to say, the advent of an Avatar is a rare occurrence.

Ram Leela is a 9 day celebration culminating in the symbolic return of Sita, wife of Lord Rama, the heroic embodiment of righteousness, from the clutches of the evil demon Ravanna, thus symbolizing the triumph of good over evil. It is also the one day of the year when the Maharaja of Benares, still popular although without governing power since 1947, presents himself in procession to his former subjects.

History, tradition and luck seemed to have conspired to show us another of the timeless aspects of life in India that St. Issa was exposed to during the six years he lived in this region.

We arrived in the vicinity of the Maharaja's summer palace just as the procession was about to begin. The streets, trees and rooftops were layered with people. The mid-afternoon sun was intense, luckily much of the avenue was shaded by large trees. We found ourselves about a quarter of a mile from the palace, so we began to inch in its direction. We reached a bridge covering a dry moat leading to the main gate where men were milling about in various kinds of uniforms. No one seemed to be giving or taking directions, so we walked on in. Inside, the huge rectangular courtyard, lined with the faded and crumbling stucco walls of the palace, was the staging ground for the parade.

Again, it was like stepping back into a past age, several in fact, like successive layers of a time capsule. Here were the Maharaja's attendants wearing starched white jodhpurs and matching jackets, knee boots, and bright orange sashes at the waist with matching turbans flamboyantly tied so one end stood straight up like a tassle of feathers while the other end hung down their backs. There were open carriages with garlanded crystal lanterns drawn by horses with silver blinders perfectly suited to Queen Victoria. At one point a camel galloped past wearing remnants of a once intricately woven headdress, now mostly colorful tatters.

It must have saddened the Maharaja to have only four elephants for the parade when his predecessors had herds numbering in the thousands. These four were decorated with colorfully painted designs, silver rings on their tusks, and faded silk blankets over their immense backs. As the parade was about to begin they knelt, allowing their trainers, called mahouts, to mount and straddle their necks just behind the huge bulge of their foreheads.

The Maharaja's personal mount was clearly the largest and most elaborately decorated. As the parade began he emerged from an inner courtyard in stately splendor with his master aboard, a band of uniformed soldiers walking alongside. Not only was he carrying the Maharaja in a howdah (throne) with gold sphinx figures on either side and a tasselled umbrella for shade, he was preceded by men waving plumed fans and he wore a hulking crown of his own.

The parade was led by a band of more ancient seeming folk musicians playing horns, flutes and kettle drums, and the characters of the pageant dated in significance, attitude and appearance from a time before written history. After three miles through the hot sun, the procession ended at a field in front of enormous papier mache demons which were to be burned in a flaming triumph of good over evil. At the signal from the Maharaja a torch was laid at the base and the crowd cheered as the demons got their just reward.

43

In Benares everything along the river faces east, not due to any superstition about the rising sun, but because the Ganges is so wide a bridge could not be built to span it until the 19th Century, and by that time the city was several thousand years old. The east bank is flat, marshy and barren, while the west bank is crowded with buildings of many ancient styles.

Among and between the buildings are the ghats, steps leading to the water which have allowed centuries of pilgrims, including St. Issa, to approach the river no matter how high or low the tide. The ghats are vital to those who come for prayers and ablutions. Some live in the city and come daily, some come from far away for the pilgrimage of a lifetime, and others come to die, be cremated and have their ashes immersed in these waters. At Benares the river is wide, fast and in spite of what goes into it daily, considered to be pure.

Sunrise is the river's time, when all movement in the city comes toward it. Later in the morning it releases its pilgrims to return to the city and their daily activities. It was not yet sunrise when we arrived at the ghat where boatmen wait for passengers. The sinking feeling I got as we stepped aboard our chosen vessel was partly because it was still dark and things were unfamiliar, and partly because the water seeped through cracks in the rickety wooden rowboat, rose around my ankles, and the boat descended measurably into the water.

We were at the southern end of the city and our boatman had to row hard against the current. As the sun began to ascend, throwing bands of light across the water and against the ghats, it became possible to see, as had Issa, the all but silent activity taking place around us at the water's edge. Everywhere there were people, men, women and children of all ages at the water's edge murmuring prayers, chanting scripture and performing bathing rites. Some would glance up at the intruders, but for most of them we did not exist. We were impressed by their ability to create a sense of privacy in the midst of a crowd, even with tourists floating by. It seemed we had been given a rare opportunity to look through a window into the past, to see a living tradition that had changed very little since the beginning of Benares, known to the ancients as Varanasi, one of the world's oldest cities.

One sight brought us back to the present. It was a man walking down the steps wearing a white cloth wrapped around his lower torso called a dhoti. He was wearing shoes and carrying his shirt and briefcase. He appeared to be going to his office, but not before his morning prayers at the river.

Another sight was a woman kneeling on what had been the terrace of a temple, now sunk up to its second story level in water. She was cleaning her oil lamp and the utensils used in her puja (worship ceremony), totally oblivious to anything but her task.

Further on was a temple which had once stood proudly at the river's edge, but now could only tilt crazily out of the water that had eroded its foundation and covered all but its dome. At some places there were trees growing in the ruins, at others, stone tigers strutted along sunken balconies while the current lapped at their feet.

Most visitors take the early morning boatride to see the burning ghats, where the dead are cremated before their ashes are given to the river. Nowhere is the difference between east and west more clearly reflected than in the attitude toward death. In the west death is feared because it is unknown, because it is so final, and because it is the ultimate threat.

We cannot understand the Vedantic view of death without comprehending its view of life. Life is the divine attribute of the human soul which is one with God, and all creation. Each soul is one with this divine principle. The human body is a vehicle for the evolution of the individual soul from the delusion that we are separate from God, through the myriad stages of growth and spiritual development, to the eventual and inevitable goal of union with God. When this goal is reached it is called self-realization, realization not as a mental process that affects only the intellect, but the experience of knowing that the Self is one with God and then realizing it, making it real and manifesting this divine Self in every waking moment.

As with any type of vehicle, the body is useful for a certain part of the journey. When the terrain changes and the present body is no longer suitable, a new one is necessary. In this view, our physical bodies are temporary vehicles. We must learn to master our body and then use it for the journey toward our spiritual goal, rather than let the desires of the body dictate and control us.

Time is the body of God and we move through it in stages called lifetimes. Death of the body is not perceived as the end of life, but as moving on to the next stage of spiritual growth which has been determined by our actions in this life. What we have put forth returns to us in precise measure; the loving receive love, the truthful reap truth, the tyrants become the tyrannized. Sorrow at the death of a loved one becomes a passing emotion which evolves into peace because of the knowledge that the beloved is continuing a passage that is the natural consequence of birth. The principle of life belongs not to the body but to the soul, and life continues even as it moves beyond our sight. Understanding this principle allows one to live, conscious of the goal, without fear.

In Issa's time these ideas were part of the ancient tradition of India and were found in the Middle East, in Palestine, Egypt and Greece.

Our boatman continued the struggle of rowing against the powerful current until we had passed most of the waterfront, then he turned the boat around and let it glide effortlessly on the current back to our starting point.

Chapter VIII

JESUS, SAINT ISSA AND THE SCIENCE OF YOGA

In the course of our research we discovered an article about the lost years written by the late Swami Sivananda of the Divine Life Society of Rishikesk. Rishi-kesh, 160 miles north of New Delhi, means land of the Rishis, those inspired sages to whom the hymns of ancient Vedic scriptures were revealed directly by God. For years we had heard stories about the Rishis and the Sadhus, wandering renunciates who live in the hills and ashrams, comparable to western monasteries, of the area.

One of the largest and most well known ashrams is the Divine Life Society Ashram situated on the west bank of the river. Approached on foot from the road by a steep flight of stairs, it consists of many large, well constructed buildings placed around inner courtyards and open areas on the terraced hillside. It was founded by the late Swami Sivananda who is revered as one of the great modern spiritual teachers of India. Dick and I had met and come to know two of his disciples, Swami Venkatesananda who was his master's private secretary for over 20 years, and Swami Chidananda who succeeded his teacher as head of the Divine Life Society.

Swami Venkatesananda agreed to talk with us about the lost years. He began by quoting from a book of Sivananda's writings.

47

The Jesus Mystery

At the age of 13 Jesus left home and returned when he was 31 years old. During his absence, he traveled throughout India, where he practiced yoga. After his return home he preached for about two years and then passed into the great beyond. Jesus arrived at the Indus River in the company of merchants, he visited Benares, Rajgriha and other holy cities, spending several years in Hindustan. He had a spirit of burning renunciation and dispassion, living as a Buddhist or Hindu monk as he assimilated the ideals, principles and precepts of Hinduism, that is why so much similarity exists between His teachings and those of Hinduism and Buddhism.

Being a perfect yogi, Lord Jesus could perform miracles. He stopped the waves of the sea, gave sight to the blind, cured lepers through his touch, and fed a multitude of people with a single loaf of bread.

Jesus was betrayed by Judas, one of his twelve disciples. He was crucified, but accepted death with great joy in order that others might live. What a magnanimous soul!

He had learned to die cheerfully for his children. His last words are an example to the world. He said, "O Lord! Forgive those who torture and crucify me, for they know not what they do." How noble! His hands were tied to the cross and nails were driven into them. Yet, even in this state he prayed for the tormentors. What a large forgiving heart he had! The image of Jesus, an embodiment of forgiveness, continues to be worshipped by millions of people throughout the world.

Jesus taught man to overcome evil by good. His cross will remain forever the supreme example of the doctrine: "Return good for evil." He had surrendered himself completely to God, knowing that God changes the heart of the unjust through the suffering of the just.

Swami Venkatesananda then went on to reminisce about his personal experience with Swami Sivananda.

Whenever Swami Sivananda spoke of Lord Jesus, which he often did, especially during the ashram's Christmas celebrations, those who saw him and heard him speak knew that he knew that what he wrote here was true, it was his personal knowledge. Not only gained from the close study of the teachings of Jesus, which are similar to both Hinduism and Buddhism, but from direct realization of what Jesus was and is even today. Perhaps it is good to explain that Benares was at that time the holy city of Hindu learning, the best of all Hindu scholars lived in Benares, and Rajgriha was a center of Buddhist learning, and close to Benares is and was the famous Sarnath where Buddha preached his first sermon. And both Hinduism and Buddhism were in their heyday during the time of Lord Jesus.

The possibility that Swami Sivananda could "know" Jesus from his own direct experience as explained by Swami Venkatesananda may be difficult for westerners to understand. We have not yet experienced consciousness as all-pervading, we only know the segment of it our mind has cordoned off for itself.

The direct realization through which Swami Sivananda was able to perceive the truth about Jesus was made clearer to us in our discussion with Swami Chidananda at Rishikesh.

Swami Chidananda has been the head of the Divine Life Society since his master died in 1963. After our arrival he invited us into a long narrow room with windows facing east toward the river which appeared to serve as an office and reception room. The three of us sat at the far end, he behind a desk piled with correspondence and books. There was a silent moment when we could hear the birds outside in the trees and the cars that occasionally passed below on the narrow road that followed the river farther north into the mountains. Then, in measured tones of deep reverence, Swami Chidananda began to speak.

"The voice of Jesus is, verily, the voice of the eternal being. Through Him is expressed the call of the infinite to the finite, the call of the cosmic being to the individual, the call of God to man. His divine voice is the same, therefore, as the voice of the Vedas and Upanishads, the voice of the Koran, the Zendavesta, Dharmapada and all such scriptures of the great religions of the world. Essentially the gospel that he preached is at one with the gospel expounded through these holy books. It is the way of denying the flesh and asserting the spirit.

"You wanted to know what exactly Swami Sivananda, my great spiritual master said, what he meant when he said that Jesus Christ was a great yogi. Is that not your query?

"When Swami Sivananda said Christ was a great yogi he meant that Jesus Christ was an adept in the science of mystical meditation, he was an adept in the science of Raja Yoga, which is the classical science of meditation expounded by the great sage Patanjali. The aphorisms, the yoga aphorisms of Patanjali are, even to this day, the ultimate authority of this science of meditation. It is a science based upon the control of the senses, the restraint and regulation of the breath and the subtle, inner vital force, and the gradual disciplining of the mind so that it is trained to gradually become indrawn.

"It is withdrawing the mind from its outgoing tendency, from its state of being dispersed amongst the outer objects of this external universe and changing its direction, thus disciplining it to become internalized, gradually mastering its constant restless movement so that the thought processes become conquered, and a state of absolute one-pointed concentration is brought about in the mind. And this concentrated mind is focused upon the ultimate reality, the inner object of our meditation, so that when, through continuous and persevering efforts one is able to bring about a continuous flow of the concentrated mind upon this one specific focal point, one enters into a state of meditation. And through meditation, ultimately, the mind is transcended.

"The mind becomes no-mind, as it were, the mind is transcended and one attains to a state of supra-mental super-consciousness where one is oblivious of the other surroundings. One transcends body consciousness, is completely dead to the senses and the body, and one attains to a state of illumined spiritual consciousness, super-consciousness which is called samadhi. In the state of samadhi, one, transcending mind and intellect, ascends upon the mystical, as it were, and attains to a state of illumination, divine illumination. One becomes liberated from the trammels of senses, body, mind and the little ego consciousness.

"This science had been mastered by Jesus and so when master Swami Sivananda said that Christ was a great yogi, he meant that Jesus was an adept in the science of Raja Yoga, an adept in samadhi, super-consciousness and had become well established in that state of highest inner meditation and super-consciousness. That is what he meant."

Swami Chidananda spoke again, "To continue this topic of Raja Yoga, Raja Yoga is also called Astanga Yoga or Patanjali's yoga. Astanga Yoga, because it has eight states of discipline,* the ultimate being the state of Samadhi, and Patanjali Yoga because Patanjali is the founder of it. Because Jesus was a master of this science, all the miracles that He performed during his public life and spiritual ministry in the holy land were the result of yogic powers that accrue to a master yogi, an adept who has ascended the highest state and so these powers are called siddhis and they comprise powers by which one has control over internal as well as external nature. One has control over the elements and one has control of life and death, as it were, and what seems impossible is possible to such a master.

"There are the lesser super-natural powers as well as the

---

*YAMA, moral conduct, NIYAMA, religious observances, ASANA, right posture, PRANAYAMA, control of prana (Subtle life force), PRATYAHARA, withdrawal of the senses from external objects, DHARANA, concentration, DHYANA, meditation, and SAMADHI, superconscious experience.

greater super-natural powers. An adept in Raja Yoga becomes possessed of these greater super-natural powers called maha-siddhis (great siddhis). So this is how we in India are able to understand the extraordinary miraculous powers which Jesus demonstrated during His life and during His ministry. And this does not cancel the possibility or deny the probability of His having these powers spontaneously, due to His divinity.

"So, being a divine descent, it is just possible that He was born with these powers. They were to Him natural and spontaneous, the only thing is He withheld manifesting them until His time had come, until the correct hour had struck, then only He manifested these powers. Otherwise, He wanted to be like any ordinary person, to fulfill the laws of the normal human plane. So that is why His life seems to be ordinary until a certain time. Then, suddenly there is this wonderful manifestation of powers starting from the marriage, the marriage celebration when the wine ran short and then, at the importunities of His mother Mary, He agreed, even though He felt the time had not yet come. He said, 'The hour has not come, my time has not yet come,' but the mother's importunities prevailed over His idea of right and wrong time and then He performed the miracle of turning the water into wine. From there onwards now He is being known publicly, so it is just possible that His power stems from both facts, one is that He was a master adept in the science of Raja Yoga, and, therefore, He had all these yogic powers coming to Him, and the second stemming from the fact that He, being a divine being, a descent of divinity, He might have possessed all these powers as a matter of birthright, as it were."

Dick answered, "Tell us, Swami, if the first view is correct, then it means that Jesus would almost have had to have come to India to gain the yogic training to become a master adept."

Swami Chidananda replied, "Well, as much as the yoga science was in those days confined mainly to this Indian sub-continent, and it had not yet spread beyond the shores of India, there is every possibility that Jesus might have journeyed to the Orient and acquired knowledge and training in the practice and mastery of yogic science in this land."

"Was there any other culture at the time of Jesus where He could have gained this kind of wisdom?" Dick asked.

"Yes," replied Swami Chidananda, "there were some mysteries in other places which were only found in certain rare and exceptional personalities, some prophets and some unique personalities, but not in the form of a very developed and perfectly systematized science. The technique was not developed in that way. In that way it is found to have been prevalent and extant in India right from those days onwards, even from before, as a very, very well developed science with exact and specific techniques and ashrams (hermitage-schools) in many places with many teachers practicing and imparting training."

Dick replied, "If the second position was true, that would mean that He was a full Avatar at birth, but it is said that only India has produced full Avatars." (An Avatar is the descent of God in human form, the degree of completeness is judged by the divine attributes demonstrated by the person—Rama and Krishna are considered full Avatars because they displayed all 16 qualities.)

"There is some reason in this statement because the concept of divine incarnation is not to be found anywhere else in the world, in any other religion in the world," Swami Chidananda said. "The concept of an incarnation of the divine is only an integral part, a salient and specific part of the Vedic religion and philosophy, and even here there have been only one or two full avatars. Other avatars are regarded as partial avatars. And in this it is not the quality of divinity that is held in question, but it is the degree of divine manifestation that is actually meant. So, in calling Christ a partial avatar neither His divinity is held in question, nor the authenticity and genuineness of His divinity. It means that at that time, in that particular period a full avatar was not necessary, was not called for. Jesus mainly came there as a messenger to give the spiritual message, the call to the life spiritual so that He did not need a full avatar when a partial avatar was quite adequate to fill the need of that particular area in that particular time." Smiling, he said, "I suppose it is economy in the cosmic scheme of things that He, God, just sends what is needed."

"In that case, Swamiji," I asked, "did Jesus incarnate because of the need of the people at that time or because He was fulfilling His own spiritual destiny?"

The Swami replied, "You see, most of these incarnations here in India came when unrighteousness had gone beyond limits, beyond bounds, and the world was plunged into a state of grave distress, so there was travail, and righteousness had to be re-established. In that time a full avatar was needed for the destruction of certain evils, so the avatar was fulfilling his destiny in the sense that his destiny was to answer the needs of beings, of human society, at that time."

"Was it the need of the people of that time to crucify Jesus?" I wondered aloud.

"It is still a puzzle to me why that was done at all," the Swami answered. "His words had the power, so even without His being crucified I'm sure His disciples would have carried out His mandate. I believe the crucifixion was done due to the degradation of the human nature that prevailed at that time. Jesus mainly came in order to bring the call to spiritual life, to bring to them the correct sense of values and bring the message of the living life of aspiration, a spiritual aspiration and divine quest, and to establish the kingdom of righteousness, the kingdom of God, the kingdom of heaven on earth in one's own heart: the kingdom of heaven in one's own heart here on earth, not in a post mortem state of existence, but right here while they are living on earth in human society. To bring, to establish the kingdom of heaven within themselves, that was His mission. That He got crucified was maybe more as a result of the quality of the human society in which He came and gave His message, rather than fulfillment of His own destiny."

I asked, "Or maybe it was so that He would have the opportunity to have the resurrection; you cannot be resurrected without dying."

"Well," said Swami Chidananda, "if you read the gospels, it seems as though He was aware of the fate that was overcoming Him and so, after a certain struggle, he accepted it. There was a moment when He was torn between the two opposite poles of the human nature and His divine sense of mission. The agony in the garden of Gethsemane was the crucial point when this inner conflict was resolved and His higher mission prevailed."

Dick said, "Possibly the crucifixion and resurrection were necessary to insure the continuation of the message. There have been many Christian martyrs and great prophets, but none with the power Jesus had to stir mankind for 2,000 years."

"Well," said Swami Chidananda, "when a person has been crucified it means a greater sense of determination in His immediate circle of followers. When the master has died for his mission we disciples, too, now feel we should be prepared to go to the extreme point in dedicating our lives in propagating his message, even at the point of death. So, maybe it was necessary to infuse in them this ultimate fearlessness."

"Swamiji, one other question," I said. "Are you familiar with the shroud of Turin which is believed to have covered Jesus' body as he lay in the tomb after the crucifixion? We are wondering if it is possible that the imprint left on the shroud was due to the fact that Christ dematerialized his body inside the tomb and then rematerialized outside. Is dematerialization a yogic power or siddhi?"

"That is one of the yogic siddhis," the Swamiji replied, "one of the well-known yogic siddhis."

"Would it have left some emanation upon the shroud?" I asked.

Swamiji answered, "I do not know the exact inner mechanics of this dematerialization and rematerialization. It is quite possible it might have given some sort of atomic radiation or something—it is a possibility."

"It must be miraculous to see the shroud," I exclaimed.

"I have never seen the shroud," said Swamiji. "I have only seen photos, in fact I have a photograph of it."

Then Dick said, "Swamiji, thank you for seeing us and giving us so much of your time. We feel very fortunate your busy schedule placed you here at the ashram during our short visit."

Swami Chidananda said, "Yes, that was the will of God. I hope you have a gainful visit in the other parts of India where you will be. I wish that the Lord gives you all success in your quest after the truth and your attempt to bring to the people the truth and the hidden wisdom of the so-called missing period in the life of our Lord Jesus the Christ."

After our visit with Swami Chidananda we walked through the ashram and down to the river. Wide, deep, clear, and swiftly flowing as it curves out of the forests of rising Himalayan foothills, it is easy to believe the Ganges helps purify those who bathe in it. We stood on a ghat at its edge watching gypsy women with silver rings on fingers and toes, through ears and noses, doing their wash while a small motorized ferry chugged back and forth across the water. The only cars in Rishikesh are the occasional taxis bringing visitors, so the sound of a motor reverberated over the late afternoon water like a 20th Century intruder in a 12th Century setting.

While standing near the small dock we met a young woman. Her name was Sanyasima, she wore the saffron robe of a renunciate. She told us she was from Sri Lanka, but now lived at the ashram and would be happy to show us some of the interesting sights of the area. She also said we were very lucky because the next day was the one day of the year when the holy men came down from the hills for a special feast held at the Gita Bhavan ashram across the river. One of our main reasons for coming to Rishikesh had been to see these elusive hermits. We had expected to have to search them out, if we were lucky enough to see them at all. Now we found they were coming to us en masse.

We made plans to meet Sanyasima early the next morning and drive 14 miles up the river to a cave where a monk had lived out his life in solitary meditation, in one of the few places left in the world where true solitude is possible. We know from the Bible that Jesus spent 40 days and nights in the wilderness, six weeks alone! Perhaps this strength in him had been nurtured by the Jains at the caves of Khandagiri and fostered by the rishis so like those meditating now in the hills around us.

The cave, known as the Cave of Vasishta after a great sage of Hindu scriptures, had been occupied by many sages and monks of the past. One of the most recent was Swami Purushotamananda, who lived there for over 30 years. When he was a young man of 27 his guru is said to have read his palm and predicted that much of his life would be spent in solitary meditation.

From the road the cave is approached down a rather steep winding path through a garden with unexpectedly rare plants and trees. These were planted by the Swami during his years here and are now cared for by the men who attend the grounds. As we descended the path we were met by a caretaker who welcomed us and then went to prepare tea to serve after we had visited the cave.

This was a natural cave, as opposed to those at Khandagiri which had been excavated from the rocks, and extended some 50 feet into the side of the mountain. The sun was overhead and the entrance comfortably large so there was plenty of light inside. The first room was empty. At its far end it narrowed and a step descended through a narrow opening into the next chamber. Here the light was dimmer but sufficient to see we were standing in an ample room, perhaps 14 x 25 feet, which was bare except for the objects of worship situated on a ledge about two feet from the ground in an alcove at the far end of the cave. There was a metal bar stretching between the walls of the alcove which were about four feet apart, and from the bar hung a brass object which, when properly outfitted with oil and wick, became a lamp. On the ledge almost directly beneath the lamp was what appeared to be a natural rock formation which was the setting for a large egg-shaped stone called a linga.

The linga is worshipped as a symbol of the unmanifested divinity, God, which is eminent in all of creation. It is the symbol of the universal into which all particulars merge, from which all particulars emerge, and is worshipped by the followers of Shiva. This particular linga appeared to be a large naturally formed granite stone in the shape of an egg. Draped around the stone was a delicate garland of small white flowers. Just to the left was a small ivory statue of Lord Shiva, also garlanded.

The cave was empty except for these three objects, the lamp, the Shiva linga and the image of Lord Shiva. The vibrations were palpable, almost visible. The outside world no longer existed, even the rarified atmosphere of the surrounding mountains was shut out. The only sound was the beating of one's heart, which gradually slowed and diminished in volume, the coursing of blood through one's veins, and the occasional rumbling of a stomach still digesting breakfast. Within moments these personal sounds faded and we were left in a stillness that enveloped and cradled us in a sense of homecoming, not to a place but to a state of serenity and wholeness that was instinctively recognized but not consciously remembered.

Perhaps this was a taste of the solitude necessary to reach so deeply inside oneself that the divine spark at one's core becomes apparent and flares like a torch to illuminate, warm and fill every crevice of the mind and heart with a sense of the almighty. Perhaps this is what the Bible calls the peace that passeth all understanding.

After some time we returned to the garden to find the caretaker waiting with fresh tea.

The river curves at that spot and the wide bank is covered with large glacial boulders which have been deposited over the ages from the high mountains above. We started to climb over them to reach the water, but stopped when we saw a solitary figure at the river's edge. A monk stood naked as he washed his robe and laid it on the rocks to dry while he bathed in the freezing torrent. This was his place and we didn't want to intrude with our presence.

Returning to Rishikesh we realized we had been gone longer than planned because as we crossed on the ferry to the opposite side of the river we saw coming toward us a streaming mass of saffron robes, sadhus of all descriptions. The feast was over and they were now returning to the hills. Fortunately, the small ferry boat only carried 20 or so at a time so the rest were milling about on the landing and the adjacent ghats, providing a field day for us as photographers.

The common denominator was the faded orange they all wore signifying their renunciation of the possessions of the material world and their dedication to the one-pointed pursuit of the experience of God.

Many wore only a piece of fabric around the waist and lower body, a loincloth similar to the garment in which Jesus is depicted while on the cross. They were young, old, clean shaven, bearded. Some wore their hair in a top knot, some had shaved heads, others had the waist-long matted locks of a sect which never cut their hair. Many wore rudraksha malas, a strand of 108 large auspicious seeds used to count the number of times a prayer or mantra is repeated, much the same as a rosary.

Some were barefoot, some wore sandals, we even saw one sadhu wearing tennis shoes. Since they were wandering monks they carry their few possessions with them, usually limited to some kind of vessel for food or water. But there was an occasional pair of glasses, umbrella, walking stick, knapsack, shawl or musical instrument such as tambourine or reed flute. Some spoke quietly to one another, one seated himself under a nearby tree and played his tambourine as he chanted, others stood silently watching the ferry boat traipse back and forth across the current.

What must it be like to live like this? Probably the closest most of us come is a brief vacation where we live out of one suitcase but have our comforts provided by hotels, campgrounds or hospitable friends. We rarely even speculate on the inner resources necessary to the kind of self-sufficiency required to live in the mountains as these men do, or in the wilderness as Jesus did for long periods of time. Where would we be without our heating and air conditioning, without super markets, and continuous stimulation from entertainment of various kinds, and where would we be without the possessions which speak in shorthand, announcing to others our value and our worth? Of course, these men don't have to worry about taxes, inflation or mortgage payments. And, we saw no fat sadhus.

While watching this panorama go by, sensing the freedom they live with, not the freedom to satisfy their desires but freedom from desires, it occurred to me that the things we believe are necessary in order for us to feel good only get in the way of our innate ability to do so.

The crowd thinned out and we wandered along the bank towards the Gita Bhavan, a series of temple buildings extending for several hundred yards along the east bank of the river. Bhavan means house or mansion and Gita refers to the Bhagavad Gita, probably the most well known to Westerners of all the Vedic scriptures. It is the dialogue between God in the form of Lord Krishna and his devotee Arjuna on the Kurukshetra battlefield through which the Lord conveys to Arjuna the essential principles and teachings of all the scriptures, and by so doing leads him from despair to the realization, "My delusion is dissolved; I have become aware of My Reality, which is God."

With these thoughts in the air we ferried back across the Ganges along with the last of the sadhus and returned to the ashram to collect our things and say goodbye.

The river Ganges as it flows through Benares (Varanasi).

Elephants in the Ram Leela Parade at Benares.

The east bank of the Ganges at Rishikesh.

Swami Chidananda, of the Divine Life
Society, Rishikesh.

Wandering holy men of
Rishikesh.

Chapter IX

ORNAMENTS OF THE UNIVERSE

One of Jesus' earliest recorded miracles was, as Swami Chidananda said, the incident at the wedding in Cana when Mary asked him to turn the water to wine and, after a brief hesitation, he complied.* Neither Jesus or Issa ever married.

The legend says Issa left his father's house before a marriage could be arranged for him. Then, as now, weddings, the matings of souls, are major events in our lives, with depths of significance we seldom fully comprehend.

During our travels in search of the lost years we were invited to the celebration of a Hindu wedding in New Delhi. Marriage practices in the east and middle east are still based on historic customs, so this was another opportunity for us to look into the past, even though some of the trappings had obviously been modernized.

The orthodox religious ceremony had taken place earlier in the day and now the two families were gathered, each at a separate location with a large contingent of guests. We had been invited by the bride's family so we joined them in the garden of a popular hotel to be fed delicacies and listen to

---

*John 2:1-11. This incident would seem to indicate Mary already knew of Jesus' miraculous abilities which raises the question of how she came to know about them.

the musicians who strolled under the flashing colored lights that had been laced through the trees. At the properly auspicious moment, very likely determined by the family pundit or astrologer, the two groups began the procession towards the Grand Oberoi Hotel a few blocks away. The flower bedecked white horse traditionally ridden by the groom was now a white Chevrolet Impala convertible, proceeding at a walking pace so that friends and family, musicians and torch bearers could walk alongside.

A special wing of the hotel had been reserved for the festivities and the families came together like the merging of two glitteringly festive rivers. The music crescendoed, the bride and groom met. She, beautiful in her ornate sari and best jewels, he, somewhat chagrined yet enjoying his spot at the center of attention. They garlanded each other with ropes of roses and then stood bashfully as photographers snapped and grandmothers clucked happily on the sidelines.

These were sophisticated young Indians who became suddenly shy and acquiescent in the face of pressure to uphold their family religious customs in such a formal, public manner. Theirs was a traditional wedding but a fairly modern courtship, at least they had met before the ceremony.

The legend says:

> When Issa was thirteen years old, the age at which an Israelite is expected to marry, the modest house of his industrious parents became a meeting place of the rich and illustrious, who were anxious to have as a son-in-law the young Issa, who was already celebrated for the edifying discourses he made in the name of the All-Powerful.

> Then Issa secretly absented himself from his father's house; left Jerusalem, and, in a train of merchants, journeyed toward the Sindh, with the object of perfecting himself in the knowledge of the word of God and the study of the laws of the great Buddhas. [1]

Ancient marriage customs seem strange and archaic to us now because we have little awareness of the context in which they were practiced. Thirteen definitely seems to be too young, however, boys in Palestine passed into manhood at this age, so marriage was the next step. Also, at the time of Jesus the average life span of an individual is thought to have been around 35 years.

Throughout the world marriages were, with very few exceptions, if any, arranged by the families of the bride and groom. It was not until the Middle Ages in Europe that the idea of romance, the idealization of the loved one, the fantasy of the perfect lover, the fairytale knight or princess, began to seep into general consciousness.

I was single the first time I came to India and when I learned arranged marriages were not only practiced but common, I was stunned. I mean, this was the 20th Century! It was not until I began to have a greater perspective of life in a spiritual context, and became less attached to my own fairytale fantasies of romance that I could relax enough to give it some thought.

More than anything, one woman conveyed to me the essence of the Vedantic concept of marriage and helped me to understand it in the context of the four stages of life in Hindu thought. She conveyed it because she had lived it with the understanding of the spiritual goal of life, and she exhibited the inner peace and contentment, the happily ever after, I had thought only came from the fulfillment of romantic dreams.

She explained the four stages of life were: (1) student, the time of preparation, (2) householder, the time of work and family obligations, (3) retirement and contemplation, and (4) the stage of religious mendicancy or renunciation.

Her life and that of her husband had been models of the tradition. Their marriage was arranged by their families and they were married at a young age. For the years their children were growing they not only were householders, but were active with Mahatma Gandhi in the political movement which later brought India its freedom from British rule. When their children were grown and established, her husband retired and they both took up contemplation of the spiritual life. After some years of this more quiet life, her husband decided it was time for him to renounce the world and live as a monk.

Since tradition decrees a husband or wife can only leave the family with the full permission of his or her spouse, it was her decision to allow him to leave and to remain with the family herself. He then joined a monastery. After some years at the monastery, he renounced even that attachment and went into the mountains to live the solitary life of the wandering sadhu or holy man. Meanwhile, his wife lived with the family of one of the children and pursued her spiritual life within the structure of her family. While her husband was a monk at the ashram his family visited him, however, after he left the ashram for the forest, they never saw him again.

It has taken me much time to come to an understanding of this way of life. I now know that once we experience our connection with God as our only unchanging relationship, we can see our relationships with each other with some perspective. Other people are not here for our convenience, our security, or to fulfill our fantasies. They each have a spiritual destiny, as do we. We come together to learn about ourselves, our reactions, our natures. How often do we seem to be drawn to a succession of partners with the same or familiar traits? Many people eventually come to see that each new partner was essentially the same as the last. What is hard to accept is that we attract partners to us who bring out the qualities we need to understand and change. So, in a sense, it is futile to go from one partner to another when the changes must eventually occur within ourselves.

With this observation in mind the question becomes, what is the difference between the old system of choosing a partner and the new? It seems we all live out our lives on two levels, the first being that of attitudes and opinions so basic, even subconscious, that we don't think about them or realize that they are not common to everyone else. It is these attitudes, imbued by family, place, tribe and religion, that we hold to so tenaciously because they are all we know. The second level is closer to the surface and is expressed through our daily habits, choices and desires.

The practice of arranged marriage brings people together with the same fundamental attitudes in the belief that with these as a firm foundation and a shared spiritual goal, the young people will be able to work out the less tightly held, more superficial areas of the relationship. Because, human nature being what it is and change being so difficult, if any adjustments are to be made and a state of balance achieved, it is certainly easier to compromise on those accessible areas close to the surface, the top soil as opposed to bedrock.

The modern attitude toward romance lets people come together in a seemingly random way, often outside the nest of family and familiar traditions, based on their ever changing surface desires and then after marriage when they clash at the deeper level, often without knowing why, and the relationship begins to flounder, they are condemned as failures.

The legend says Issa left Jerusalem with the object of perfecting himself in the knowledge of the word of God and the study of the laws of the great Buddhas, the implication being he also wanted to avoid marriage. In the Vedantic system with the four stages of life there is no need to go anywhere. Life is spirit and spirituality is manifesting daily in life, if we will only see it. The householder stage is the glue which holds society together, doing the work, raising the children, and caring for the elders. The seeds sown by the householders begin to flower and their children become self-sustaining, then the parents can devote their time to their own desire to know God.

Of course, these are ideals that few individuals live up to completely, but the society does foster them and so the spiritual life within the context of work and family is honored.

Thirteen year old Issa appears to have instinctively known that marriage is a mating not of bodies or minds, but of souls temporarily clothed in bodies and minds. He was able to see the short term desires of a physical world in relation to life's ultimate purpose.

In the legend the mature Issa returned to Jerusalem to speak eloquently about the relationship between men and women.

> *Hearken to what I say to you: Respect woman; for in her we see the mother of the universe, and all the truth of divine creation is to come through her.*

> *She is the fount of everything good and beautiful, as she is also the germ of life and death. Upon her man depends in all his existence, for she is his moral and natural support in his labors.*

> *In pain and suffering she brings you forth; in the sweat of her brow she watches over your growth, and until her death you cause her greatest anxieties. Bless and adore her, for she is your only friend and support on earth.*

> *Respect her; defend her. In so doing you will gain for yourself her love; you will find favor before God, and for her sake many sins will be remitted to you.*

> *Love your wives and respect them, for they will be the mothers of tomorrow and later the grand-mothers of a whole nation.*

> *Be submissive to the wife; her love enobles man, softens his hardened heart, tames the wild beast in him and changes it to a lamb.*

Wife and mother are the priceless treasures which God has given to you. They are the most beautiful ornaments of the universe, and from them will be born all who will inhabit the world.

Even as the Lord of Hosts separated the light from the darkness, and the dry land from the waters, so does woman possess the divine gift of calling forth out of man's evil nature all the good that is in him.

Therefore I say unto you, after God, to woman must belong your best thoughts, for she is the divine temple where you will most easily obtain perfect happiness.

Draw from this temple your moral force. There you will forget your sorrows and your failures, and recover the love necessary to aid your fellow-men.

Suffer her not to be humiliated, for by humiliating her you humiliate yourselves, and lose the sentiment of love, without which nothing can exist here on earth.

Protect your wife, that she may protect you — you and all your household. All that you do for your mothers, your wives, for a widow, or for any other woman in distress, you will do for your God. [2]

Chapter X

TO BE BORN AGAIN

Before leaving for India we wrote to Gopi Krishna, the well-known author on Kundalini Yoga who lives in Kashmir's capitol city of Srinigar, and so the possibility of meeting him to discuss the travels of Saint Issa plus the mystique of the mountains themselves was the only encouragement necessary for us to make a detour over the southern-most rim of the Himalayas and down into the legendary vale of Kashmir.

India is often called a nation of villages, but it was not until we flew north out of New Delhi that this became apparent. The first part of the hour-long flight was at relatively low altitudes so we were able to get a clear view of the landscape, that area of the Punjab called the Indo-Gangetic Plain. In some places it is a 200-mile wide trough, originally as deep as 6,500 feet, which originated at the same time as the earth buckled and lifted up the Himalayas. In the last few million years the rivers running out of the mountains have dumped mud and stones, gradually filling up the immense trench, creating fertile soil for farming.

From the air hundreds of villages seemed to be set out like marbles on a Chinese checkerboard. Each village had two or three short roads fanning out in different directions to connect it with the surrounding hamlets. The tightly woven pattern of village-road-village-road extended in all directions as far as the eye could see. The thought of Saint Issa crossing these great plains on foot, not only once but a second time on his return as well, suddenly drew him into focus as not only one of wisdom and saintliness, but a man of awesome strength and determination.

The address we had for Gopi Krishna took us to a three story stone house where we were greeted by a young girl who explained her grandfather was upstairs with a visitor and would see us shortly.

As a young man, Gopi Krishna dutifully performed his daily meditation. In 1937, after seventeen years of this discipline, he had an experience he has since written about as the classic awakening of the yogic kundalini energy.

In the ancient scientific practice of yoga, it is believed that each individual possesses latent divine energy. This energy is symbolized as a serpent coiled at the base of the spine which, when awakened through meditation and spiritual practices, will rise along the spine, activating seven centers of energy called chakras.

In his autobiography, "Kundalini, the Evolutionary Energy in Man," Gopi Krishna described what he experienced of this energy.

> There was sound like a nerve thread snapping and instantaneously a silvery streak passed through the spinal cord, exactly like the sinuous movement of a white serpent in rapid flight, pouring an effulgent, cascading shower of brilliant energy into my brain, filling my head with a blissful luster.

In the forty years since that day, Gopi Krishna has observed and recorded his experiences, and has made a systematic study of this phenomenon and its history throughout Indian philosophical traditions and all world religions. He now believes the process is complete and has released his writings about this research and the phenomenon he feels is a manifestation of the fundamental bio-energy of life, the energy which creates genius, and is the connection between the inner and outer realities. His work has gained the interest of scientists in Europe and the United States as well as India.

After the other visitors left we were invited upstairs to join Gopi Krishna for tea.

When asked about the Tibetan legend found by Notovitch and the possibility that Jesus had come to India as a young man, he said:

"You see, about spiritual matters legends grow, and probably spiritual men provide the most fertile area for rumors, legends, stories, tales and such things. I am not sure if he came to India, but in his teachings there is that esoteric wisdom that has been known in India for thousands of years. For instance, this doctrine of rebirth. This rebirth is a very important part of Indian faith because the two higher castes among Hindus are called the twice born, that is, they are born twice. And by this is meant the spiritual birth, the entry into a new life of spirit. Jesus refers to that, and that is an Indian concept. There has been a similar thing in Egypt also about the second birth, but the doctrine is mainly Indian.

"So, I can't say whether it was from the Indian sources that he got this, or if it was his own inner intuition, but in any case there is an esoteric link between Jesus and Indian principles. And during those days there was a great interchange of ideas, especially in spiritual matters, between India and the Occident. India has been the cradle of methods of yoga and spiritual ideas from very ancient times, and so, naturally, he must have imbibed some of that teaching, either here or there."

Srinigar was beautiful in its nest beside the river Jhelum, and Dal Lake was invitingly edged with exotic houseboats for hire, but our destination was Gulmarg, a former British hill station on the far western rim of the mountains. Issa had escaped into mountains like these. If we couldn't climb the same stones, we could at least try reaching equivalent heights.

The highway out of the city was straight and well-maintained. On either side rich fields were being harvested by women bundling huge stacks of grain which were then hoisted over their men's backs so they could be trundled along the highway and back to the villages. All we really could see of this process were brown skinned legs and feet extending below the haystacks we met shimmying alongside us on the road.

After an hour the road began to climb through timbered foothills and after ascending many miles and several thousand feet the car came to a stop at a wide spot in the road where men were standing holding the reins of small horses. We put on our coats and got out to stretch our legs and look around. Before we knew it our luggage and camera equipment had been slung on the backs of two ponies which were being led off on a trail that disappeared around the side of a hill. The other ponies were for us to ride since cars were not allowed beyond that point.

Feeling somewhat guilty because the ponies were so small, we mounted and docilely held on as a slight man with bronze, leathery skin, wearing only a light sweater over a cotton shirt led us off on the rocky path following our luggage.

It was now late afternoon and beginning to grow quite cold as we approached the rambling wooden structure of the Highlands Park Hotel. To reach our room in one of the outlying cabins we walked through a garden of summer's last flowers, enormous and colorful, whose fragrances vied with the aroma of the pine trees and that incredibly fine mountain air. What bliss for the lungs after the heat and congestion of Calcutta, Benares, and New Delhi. We made arrangements for a guide to meet us the next morning, and after dinner in what was a former British outpost Officer's Club, and an evening walk through the gardens, we turned in.

The guide met us early the next morning. We had not come prepared for mountain hiking so he brought several pair of sturdy high-top laced shoes for us to try on. At this point I was wearing almost all the clothes I had brought from New Delhi, two pairs of slacks, three pairs of socks, a blouse, two pullover sweaters, a silk scarf, a heavy coat and a wool shawl over all that.

Our destination was the glacial lake at the top of a mountain called Al Pather, a mere 3,000 vertical feet from the hotel.

The trail began a few hundred yards from our cabin and there, waiting patiently for two extremely green mountaineers were three ponies, one for each of us and one for the guide. Two bearers were waiting to carry lunch and the camera equipment. These bearers, or pony wallahs, care for the ponies and conduct tourists up the mountain in summer. In winter they become sled wallahs and push/pull visitors around on sleds over the ice and snow covered trails. And, unbelievable as it may sound, that cold fall morning as we started out on a day long trek up the side of a rock-covered mountain, they were barefoot!

The first hour took us through a beautifully forested area. The sun had risen past the towering mountains on the eastern rim of the Vale of Kashmir and now, as we worked our way up the western side, it came filtering through the trees to caress the moss covered ground like a hesitant lover. The music of the freshly melted glacial water in the streams we forded could not compete with the almost orchestral beauty of the birds' song as we passed beneath them.

The trees began to thin out as we came closer to the timber line and then, as if held back by an unseen hand, they stopped their advance and we were faced with an unimpeded view of the next 2,000 rocky feet to our destination.

Just when we were about to stop and reconsider the whole idea we reached a strategically placed rest stop where we were offered that bracing remnant of the British raj, mid-morning tea. And, wonder of wonders, for the first time in weeks, so our guide told us, the clouds retreated to reveal not only a brilliant blue sky, but the entire Northern Himalayan range. We could now see the valley laid out below us and the mountains which delineate its farthest rim, including the immense Nanga Parbat—26,600 feet high, 60 miles to the north.

After tea, a brief rest and a flurry of picture taking, we remounted our little horses and began to ascend the steep switch-back trail to the top of our particular mountain. Fortunately, its 14,000 feet made it almost incidental in comparison with the "real" mountains we now saw all around us. I appreciated our feat more when I later realized that Mount Blanc, the highest peak in western Europe, is only 15,781 feet high.

As we rose higher and higher along the trail, the ponies stepping perilously close to the edge and the stones they displaced with their hooves tumbling forever over the side, it became a form of mental self-preservation to look out, instead of down.

At some point we acquired an escort of circling birds who followed our progress, undoubtedly amazed at how slow we were when they could soar above and beyond us with such ease.

Finally the ponies could go no further and so after climbing the last half mile on foot over immense boulders, we reached the glacial lake. Our triumph was duly recorded by posing for pictures at the water's edge and we celebrated by devouring the box lunches from the hotel.

A day near the top of the world cannot really be described in words because the sights, smells and sounds evoke more than feelings. I can't say now what I had expected, but after reading about the Himalayas, about the saints and yogis who reached enlightenment there, I know I expected something unique, certainly different, something to make these mountains more spiritual than any other, some visible difference which could have caused the revelations experienced by so many.

What I had seen was beautiful but not really that different from the Sierra Nevada I had hiked through as a child with my father, or the Alps I skied later. Stone was stone, ice melted, and the water collected in streams which flowed downhill. Wildflowers grew facing the sun. The laws of nature required obedience in Kashmir just as they did on the other side of the earth in California.

From that moment enlightenment was no longer a function of place, it could happen anywhere.

The clouds had returned during lunch and our guide was anxious to leave so we could be sure to reach the hotel before dark. We followed the same trail down but this time, because much of the distance was too steep for the ponies to descend carrying passengers, we got to walk/stumble/slide down the rocky surface. We reached the hotel exhilarated, exhausted and happy.

The following morning we mounted our ponies for the last time and trekked back over the path to the road where our driver found us waiting for the ride back to Srinigar.

The next stop on our search was Amritsar from where we would travel by bus to Dharamsala, the present home in India of the Dalai Lama, former religious and secular ruler of Tibet. Because the legend of Saint Issa had been found in that mystical land, we wanted to ask Tibetan scholars what they might know of it. Also, we were eager to see and film practices of Tibetan Buddhism.

Airport security procedures at Srinigar are especially tight because of the proximity to Pakistan, so after we were cleared we had quite a wait until all the other passengers could also be searched. One by one they came into the tourist lounge and it soon became evident we would be flying with two large groups of middle-aged American tourists.

We boarded the plane and I had just settled my camera

case under my feet, which meant my knees were up under my chin, and arranged myself as comfortably as possible when I felt a tap on my shoulder. A lady from the row behind me was leaning over the back of my seat.

"Dear," she said as she nodded sideways to her seat-mates, "we're very curious to know what you and your husband are doing here because you don't look like the rest of us?"

Trying to be noncommital because I had been looking forward to a quiet flight, I replied, "We're traveling around filming in north India."

"Oh," she brightened, "what kind of film is it?"

"A documentary."

Now she was really interested and insisted on knowing more. I began with the years missing from the Bible and lightly touched on the legend.

Just as she was gearing up for another round of questions the seatbelt sign flashed on and she had to sit down for takeoff.

The plane had just reached cruising altitude and leveled off when the lady in the seat next to me cleared her throat, put her hand lightly on my arm and said in a soft voice, "Is it really true what you just said about eighteen missing years in Jesus' life?"

With this began an hour-long conversation in which I related the Biblical omission and she told me in some detail of her recent conversion to the Charismatic movement. Her born-again experience had come at a time when she felt life was empty and unfulfilled. She was taken to a service by friends and, for the first time, saw people in an ecstatic relationship with something they called the Holy Spirit. She could not define her feelings, she only knew she felt such a deep sense of desolation at being outside the experience going on around her.

She began to attend meetings and to ask to receive the Holy Spirit. But nothing happened. After a time her persistence began to fade and she felt more hopeless than ever. Then, one day after returning from church, she felt something tell her to go back and stay there, praying, until her prayer was answered. She did, and after hours of remaining while other groups came and went, she told me with tears of memory welling in her eyes, "The Holy Spirit broke open my heart and filled it up."

She then spoke of falling to the floor sobbing and speaking in tongues, languages totally foreign to her conscious mind.

It seemed as I sat beside her that even though 18 months had passed since her initial experience, it was still affecting her strongly. But I was surprised to hear her go on to tell me about her fight with the Devil. A Devil that seemed to be not only real, but a constant, ever-nearing presence that she always had to be on guard against. This Devil inhabited parts of her mind, he was constantly battling with Jesus, and it took all the strength she could summon to avoid falling into his evil grasp.

My heart went out to this soft-spoken grey-haired lady who seemed to feel a desperate need to bare her soul and reach out for answers from a stranger on a plane.

All I could say was that for me the Devil was not an independent force out there in the world battling for my soul. I told her I felt my personal commitment to the truth, which is God, was gradually building a foundation of faith which supported all aspects of life, and, because I was relatively new at it, this foundation was stronger in some areas than in others. I told her I believed any weak spots in this foundation were caused, not by a devil or the presence of dark and evil forces, but by my own lack of awareness and faith. What was needed to overcome those weaknesses was to call on God to help fill that part of my awareness, that part of myself, with light and the presence of divinity, because the Devil is like darkness that disappears as soon as the lamp is switched on, it does not stay to do battle with the light.

The aura of sadness which had hovered about her seemed to lift a bit, and as the plane landed in Amritsar we shook hands and wished each other well. I hope she has conquered her Devil.

Amritsar, 340 miles northwest of New Delhi on the India-Pakistan border, is the major city of the Sikh religion. Sikhism was founded by Guru Nanak, a Hindu, in the 15th Century in an attempt to reconcile differences between Moslems and Hindus. He proclaimed, "There is no Moslem, there is no Hindu. There is one God, the Supreme Truth."

He was succeeded by 10 gurus and it was the 10th in this line who converted Sikhism into an almost militaristic faith whose men were instantly recognizable by five signs—an uncut beard and hair held in place by a steel comb, a steel armband on their right wrist, knee-length trousers, and a sword.

For a brief time after the end of the Mogul reign, the Sikhs had their own kingdom in the Punjab, but this was ended by the arrival of British rule. Today they are still easily recognizable by their beards and turbans.

For us Amritsar was the stopping-off point for the trip to Dharamsala, the area in the hills of North Central India, the Punjab Himalayas, provided by the Indian government for the Dalai Lama, the exile government of Tibet, and for the Tibetans who were forced to leave their homeland or remain and live under Chinese domination.

Amritsar is also the site of the famous Golden Temple of the Sikhs, unique from any other in India. We reached the temple just as the sun was beginning to set. We approached what appeared to be an open archway in the middle of a block-long two-story building, its facade lined with shops and the normal clutter of an Indian streetfront. The high tunnel-like archway served as a transition from the teeming streets outside to the atmosphere of calm reverence within.

What we noticed first was the coolness of the pale marble on our bare feet. The sun was setting and lights were being switched on. As we passed through the arch into the open interior, we saw a wide marble promenade surrounding the rectangular expanse of water, and then the temple appeared, floating like an ornate golden box on a rippling mirror.

This temple, the repository of the Granth Sahib, the most holy book of the Sikhs, is made of white marble and covered with gold leaf. Its beauty is a vivid reminder of the high culture and advanced civilization enjoyed by India in the past. It exemplifies the beauty and richness which acted as a magnet on European explorers like Christopher Columbus, enticing them to undertake treacherous voyages in hopes of discovering a shortcut to the land of wealth they called the Indies.

The temple itself is approached by walking out over the water on a marble causeway divided in the center so that approaching and departing pilgrims pass each other in silent procession.

Once inside the small building we saw men richly dressed in silks with beautiful turbans sitting on the floor continuously chanting passages from the scriptures; the amplified sound of their prayers reverberating over the water and out into the night.

As the sun continued to set, the water began to darken and the lights brightened against it in contrast. The sky to the west was full of small white puffs of clouds, giving depth and dimension to the golden expanse. This ethereal light struck the gold on the temple roof and seemed to burnish it with a warm essence before continuing on to paint its exact reflection on the surface of the water. What we saw was an unforgettable sequence of sky, temple and water joined by a shared illumination.

Gopi Krishna at his home in Srinager, Kashmir.

The Golden Temple of Amritsar.

Chapter XI

SAINT ISSA AND BUDDHISM

The legend says Issa spent six years in Jagannath, Raja-griha, Benares and the other holy cities of India. It is amazing to think that this was twice the length of time spent by Jesus during his ministry in Palestine. During this time Issa learned the language and studied the scriptures. He studied the scriptures with the priests, but did not agree with their methods of applying them. He could see the essence of the great teachings and how they had come to be distorted to benefit the priest class at the expense of large numbers of people in other segments of society.

Issa not only understood the scriptures, he lived them and taught them to those parts of society considered by the priests to be beneath concern. When the priests threatened him Issa disregarded their words and remained with the lower classes. He was tireless, compassionate, loving. He was able to teach with few and simple words. He was unthreatened by so-called authority.

In our minds Issa was growing more and more like what we knew of Jesus.

The legend says:

He declaimed strongly against man's arrogating to himself the authority to deprive his fellow beings of

84

their human and spiritual rights. "Verily," he said, "God has made no difference between his children, who are all alike dear to Him."[1]

While denying the priests' interpretation of the scriptures Issa saw their essence and taught his followers:

One law has been given to man to guide him in his actions: "Fear the Lord, thy God; bend thy knee only before Him and bring to Him only the offerings which come from thy earnings."[2]

Because he could see the one God behind the many forms used to express and experience Him, he denied the priests' interpretation of God as three-formed. He said:

The eternal Judge, the eternal Spirit, constitutes the only and indivisible soul of the universe, and it is this soul alone which creates, contains and vivifies all.

He alone has willed and created. He alone has existed from eternity, and His existence will be without end; there is no one like unto Him either in the heavens or on the earth.

The great creator has divided His power with no other being; far less with inanimate objects, as you have been taught to believe, for He alone is omnipotent and all sufficient.

He willed, and the world was. By one divine thought he reunited the waters and separated them from the dry land of the globe. He is the cause of the mysterious life of man, into whom He has breathed part of His divine Being.[3]

Those who deprive their brothers of divine happiness will themselves be deprived of it; and the Brahmins and the Kshatriyas shall become the Sudras of the Sudras, with whom the Eternal will stay forever.

In the day of judgment the Sudras and the Vaisyas will be forgiven for that they knew not the light, while God will let loose his wrath upon those who arrogated his authority.[4]

Did Jesus not say "the first shall be last and the last first"?

The white priests and the warriors (Brahmins and Kshatryas), who had learned of Issa's discourse to the Sudras, resolved upon his death, and sent their servants to find the young teacher and slay him.[5]

One wonders if Issa knew or only sensed that his purpose was not to be condemned for teaching these people, but for proclaiming the truth to his own some time in the future.

But Issa, warned by the Sudras of his danger, left by night Jagannath, gained the mountain, and settled in the country of the Gautamides, where the great Buddha Sakya-Muni came to the world, among a people who worshipped the only and sublime Brahma.[6]

Is it coincidence that one of the historically repeated traits of mankind is spiritual regeneration, or is it true as stated in the "Bhagavad Gita," that God incarnates in human form from time to time when disharmony threatens to overrun the world?

One such period of regeneration began in the 5th Century before the birth of Jesus with the birth of Gautama Buddha in the Lumbini Grove in a village in Nepal. Tradition says Buddha led the sheltered life prescribed by his birth as a prince. But upon observing the poverty, pain and illness of life outside his palace he left it, determined to learn the meaning of life. After years of austerities and meditation he attained enlightenment at Bodhgaya.

The first sermon of Gautama the Buddha was preached in the park at Sarnath where the Wheel of Law (Dharma) was set into motion and the eight-fold path to enlightenment was revealed: right views, right intention, right speech, right action, right livelihood, right effort, right mindfulness and right concentration. These were the principles which Buddha called the Middle Way, and it was to the followers of Buddha that Issa fled while escaping from the priests of Jagannath.

We had seen Sarnath on an early morning during our visit to Benares. It is only seven miles away, and we found it peaceful, almost deserted. At the time of Buddha the area was a deer park; it is often referred to as such even today. But now it is in what appears to be the process of leisurely excavation by archeologists. At the time of our visit, new areas were being uncovered and these were roped off from the visitors. A sign read:

In this park there once lived five ascetics who had previously deserted Buddha in the course of the latter's search for enlightenment. Later, when Buddha achieved enlightenment at Bodh-Gaya, he proceeded to this place to expound his new doctrine first to his former companions. Buddha thus preached his first sermon at Sarnath and laid here the foundation of the faith of Buddhism, an event commonly known to the Buddhist as Dharma Chakra pravartana, turning the "Wheel of the Law."

Like Lumbini, where Buddha was born, Bodh-Gaya, where he obtained enlightenment, and Kushin-agar, where he breathed his last, Sarnath is a holy place of pilgrimage in the Buddhist world from early times.

The visual focal point at Sarnath is the Dhamekh Stupa which, from a distance, appears as an enormous two-tiered projectile with its gently pointed tip aimed at the sky. At closer range the base is octagonal and the few remaining carved stones which apparently once covered and decorated the base share the immense surface with the scattered tufts of grass which have poked their way through the bricks.

Antiquities from the 3rd Century B.C. to the 12th Century A.D., including the symbol for modern India, a stunningly stylized marble statue of four lions on a circular base, each sitting on its haunches with forelegs erect and long curly mane majestically draped on either side of its head, are to be seen in the museum adjacent to the deer park. There is a Chinese temple and a Tibetan monastery. The Chinese temple is unique because its interior is covered with a continuous mural portraying incidents in the life of the Buddha.

In his 80th year Buddha came to Kushinagar and passed into nirvana on the banks of the river Hiranyavati. From these beginnings Buddhism spread through north India. By the 3rd Century B.C. the emperor Asoka had accepted Buddhism and taken upon himself the mission of spreading its teachings.

Asoka was the grandson of the Mauryan emperor Chandragupta. At this point in Indian history the Persians had been succeeded by the brief presence of Alexander the Great, and then the Maurayan dynasty gained prominence.

His early years of rule were conventionally military and political, however one war, the Kalinga campaign of 261 B.C., in which 100,000 were slain and 150,000 taken as slaves, became the turning point in his life. Asoka described his conversion in the following words:

> Just after the taking of Kalinga, His Sacred Majesty began to give instruction in Righteousness. When an unconquered country is conquered, people are

killed, they die, or are made captive. Thus arose His Sacred Majesty's remorse for having conquered the Kalingas. Today, if a hundredth or a thousandth part of those who suffered in Kalinga were to be killed, to die or be taken captive, it would be very grievous to His Sacred Majesty. If anyone does him wrong it will be forgiven so far as it can be forgiven.[7]

The "righteousness" of which Asoka spoke was the teaching of Gautama Buddha. During his reign, Buddhism was codified, and laws and principles of the new formal religion were established. Asoka envisioned Buddhism as a missionary faith and sent emissaries to Macedonia, Syria, Egypt, Judea and Greece, and also to the Pythagoreans in Greece and the Essenes in Judea in an attempt to convert them to his beliefs. He was successful in spreading Buddhism throughout India and Ceylon, from where it traveled to Southeast Asia and eventually covered the Far East. Through this policy King Asoka is responsible for the precepts of Buddhism being known in Palestine during the time of Issa.

Asoka put into practice his Buddhist ideals. For example, he appointed special "Officers of Righteousness," who went to all parts of the empire to oversee local officials. The officers were to make certain that local authorities promoted "welfare and happiness . . . among servants and masters, brahmans and rich, the needy and the aged." They were also responsible for preventing "wrongful imprisonment or chastisement," and for ensuring special consideration for "cases where a man has a large family, has been smited by calamity, or is advanced in years."

Emperor Asoka is perhaps most well known for the edicts written on rocks and stone pillars which are still to be found. One such pillar reads:

I have had banyan trees planted to give shade to man and beast; groves of mango trees I have had planted. I have caused wells to be dug; resthouses have been erected; and numerous watering places have been provided by me here and there for the enjoyment of man and beast.[8]

The emperor also converted to vegetarianism and fostered the spread of ahimsa, the doctrine of nonviolence. His sincerity might be noted from a proclamation on a palace menu which read:

Formerly, in the kitchen of His Sacred and Gracious Majesty, many hundreds of thousands of living creatures were slaughtered every day to make curries. But now only three living creatures are slaughtered for curry, to wit, two peacocks and an antelope—the antelope, however, not always.[9]

Asoka renounced war and preached the Golden Rule to his soldiers. He united most of the subcontinent in a reign so remarkable that H. G. Wells, in his "Outline of History," ranked him as probably the greatest ruler of all time.

Within fifty years of Asoka's death, his benevolent empire had succumbed to the quarrels and factionalism of his successors. The government inspired by Buddhist ideals faded, but the ideals themselves remained strong until the 11th and 12th Centuries A.D., when the invading forces of Islam ended the rule of Buddhism in India.

Four hundred years had passed since the time of Buddha, and two hundred years since the reign of Asoka when the legend says Issa incurred the wrath of the priests at Jagannath and left by night for the mountains of Nepal, where the followers of Buddha lived.

History does not recall the precise form of Buddhism Issa would have encountered in Nepal, but we do know that it was through Nepal that Buddhism spread north into Tibet, and we were now able to observe Tibetan Buddhism in a form which has remained virtually unchanged since 400 A.D. The isolation of Tibet has served as a time capsule, preserving customs, ritual and thought for over 1600 years, until the Chinese invasion forced the Tibetans and their religion into the outer world and the 20th Century.

The irony of this action by the Chinese being that now, instead of being confined to one remote and highly inaccessible part of the world, Tibetan Buddhism has been embraced by people in distant lands who might never have known it otherwise. It reminds me of what happens when one tries to decimate a dandelion by blowing the flower off the stem—the flower in that form may disappear but its seeds are carried on the wind to land, germinate and flower again in far greater numbers.

The Dhamekh Stupa at Sarnath, where Buddha preached his first sermon.

Chapter XII

FROM THE TOP OF THE WORLD

The bus ride from Amritsar took us through six hours of fields and foothills before finally arriving in Dharamsala. The presence of Tibetan refugees has made the area well-known so there are more visitors than in other hillside villages; it even has a tourist officer who was most helpful in making our arrangements.

From the door of his office we could see the distant tourist bungalow, a large English-style wood frame building, really a Victorian collection of turreted corner rooms with peaked roofs, verandas, and balconies set on a flat expanse of green lawn before which the hills dropped away exposing the plains beyond.

We were given a spacious octagonal corner suite. After lunch we found a telephone and made contact with a representative of His Holiness the Dalai Lama, who, when he learned of our mission, invited us to meet him the following morning at the Tibetan Library a mile and a half up the mountain.

By the time we had carried our camera equipment the short 150 yards from our room in the guest house out to the road the next morning we were breathless, and not a little bit intimidated by the fact that the road twisted out of sight into the misty overcast that surrounded us. We had been told the

Library of Tibetan Works and Archives where we were to meet a man named Sherpa Tulku was a mile and a half further up the mountains. Since we hoped to film this center of exiled Tibet, we needed all the equipment we had in our hands and slung over our shoulders. Luckily, two of the camera cases were metal so we could walk a hundred yards and then stop, sit down on them, and catch our breath. From time to time we passed old men with characteristic Tibetan features herding goats down the mountains. How strange our breathlessly puffing little caravan must have looked to people who had scaled 20,000 feet high mountains in order to escape their Chinese pursuers.

As we rounded the last curve in the road we came upon the first of the Tibetan areas we were to visit that day. This was the Library of Tibetan Works and Archives, and its surrounding compound, consisting of a number of two-story white stucco buildings which serve as residences for members of the community.

The main building is the three-story library built of white stucco. The wooden columns and railings of the veranda through which we entered were brightly painted in red, yellow and green, the broad wooden moldings around the door and the eaves beneath the overhang of the second level were intricately painted in beautifully stylized floral designs of all colors. These, combined with the flowering bushes on either side of the doorway, presented a colorful welcome.

To our surprise as we entered the building, we were met by a number of young American and European men and women. We soon found out that the scholars at the library give courses in Tibetan language, history and religion and that these fortunate students paid only a few dollars a month for instruction as well as room and board.

One of them took the message of our arrival to the appropriate place and soon we were approached by a young man who introduced himself as Sherpa Tulku, translator to His Holiness the Dalai Lama. In the course of the day in which he guided us throughout the Tibetan community, we came to appreciate more and more his flawless English—he was a graduate of Colgate University—his friendliness, helpfulness, his vast knowledge of things Tibetan, and his willingness to answer questions.

Sherpa first told us some very good news. It seems the previous night His Holiness had a dream containing certain signs indicating today was the auspicious day for the monks at the monastery adjacent to His residence to perform a ceremony called Tag Juma for the purpose of purifying the atmosphere of the monastery and surrounding villages. Dick and I looked at each other with what must have appeared as conspiratorial grins; could it be just another coincidence? Now, instead of filming buildings and occasional passing figures, we were being given an opportunity to document a rare ancient ceremony. It was to be held in the afternoon, so Sherpa suggested we visit the library, have lunch with him at the dining room for scholars and residents, and then he would arrange to have one of the jeeps drive the three of us up the mountain to His Holiness's residence.

Once these decisions were made, he ushered us into the room to the right of the spacious entrance hall. The room was lined with metal bookshelves, but before we could notice anything else, we were struck by the presence of a gleaming bronze Buddha, almost lifesize, in the center of the room. It was seated in a crosslegged meditation pose and was draped with pale orange fabric, covering all but the right shoulder and arm, which was resting on the right knee.

The hair was stylized in small curled mounds covering the head, the earlobes were long, extending almost to the shoulders, and there was a teardrop of turquoise in the center of the forehead. It was seated on two bronze pillows draped with white netting, a bouquet of cut flowers before it. At first the large, almond-shaped eyes appeared closed, but as we approached we saw they were slightly open, with a gaze that, while disregarding the presence of intruders in the room, seemed to shine with an inner experience of bliss, fulfillment and satisfaction.

In one stroke this Buddha obliterated my concept of Tibetans as resigned refugees, outcasts from their homeland, the victims of oppression. What this Buddha conveyed was that the Dharma of Tibetan Buddhism was proceeding as it must, that nothing had been lost. The statue could almost be heard to say, "God's in His Heaven, all's right with the world."

We walked around the room as Sherpa showed us the manuscripts that had been carried safely out of Tibet by caravans. They are in loose-leaf form, as were the Tibetan writings Notovitch saw. These were long rectangular pages in bundles, perhaps six inches high, wrapped in a heavy, yellow cotton fabric. The ends of the bundles which faced the edge of the bookshelves had flaps of embroidered and brocaded fabric containing caligraphy, each flap announcing the contents of that particular bundle.

Sherpa explained that the manuscripts in this room represented the repository of Tibetan scriptures which had survived the invasion of the Chinese. He also showed us box after box of microfilm, explaining that complete sets of all the writings were now preserved in various parts of the world. Never again would these treasured scriptures be threatened with extinction because only one copy existed.

After saying a silent good-bye to the compelling face of the Buddha, we climbed the stairs to the second floor of the library and followed Sherpa until we came to a doorway barred by a huge bolt and impressive padlock.

Once inside we were greeted by the benign faces of countless statues of the Buddha arranged in glass-fronted cabinets and placed on tabletops, each with a container for the fresh flowers which were changed daily. These, we learned, had all been rescued from the most important monasteries of the land when the Dalai Lama and his followers fled to India. These statues, plus the contents of the room we had just visited, comprise the largest concentration of Tibetan scripture and temple art still existing.

Lunch was simple and quick. Moo-moo, a big dumpling floating in broth, and buttered tea, Tibetan style.

Our main purpose in coming all the way up to Dharamsala had been to find out if His Holiness the Dalai Lama had any information about the legend found by Notovitch at Himis, which was once part of the far western region of Tibet.

Now, as we sat with Sherpa in the Lama's dining room, a first-floor room in a building adjacent to the library, he told us that His Holiness had been asked this question by visitors about one year ago and had replied that he had no personal knowledge of the legend. When we told Sherpa about the corroboration by Swami Abhedananda of seeing the manuscript in 1925, Sherpa suggested a search might be instituted by His Holiness for what information might still exist. Sherpa was doubtful because of the political situation in Tibet and the fact that while the Chinese had improved some conditions by building schools, roads and factories, they had also destroyed monasteries, forced lamas to marry and burned scriptures. He promised to let us know if an inquiry turned up anything.

Outside, it had begun to drizzle, so the canvas top to the jeep was put on before we drove further up the mountain.

The residence, called the Celestial Abode, of His Holiness the Dalai Lama, political and spiritual leader of Tibet until March 18, 1959, when he was forced to flee the country, is a short three miles from the library. His Holiness's residence faces a rectangular courtyard at the opposite end of which are two sets of stairs, ascending to a building with smooth wood plank floors, and interior wooden pillars rising up to the ceiling which appeared to be about twenty feet high. As we approached the main entrance we could hear chanting so low and rumbling it sounded like the movement of the earth, vibrations felt before they were heard. Soon we saw rows of monks seated facing each other to form a central aisle which led to the raised altar and the large image of Avalokiteshvara, the Bodhisattva of compassion and mercy, the patron deity of Tibet.

The monks, many of whom seemed quite young, wore red robes and played a variety of instruments. Most striking were the ten-foot-long horns, propped on stands and hung with varicolored ribbons, and what appeared to be snare drums mounted on poles and played with felt-covered mallets on gracefully curving sticks. There were also large double-hand cymbals and shorter, more highly-pitched horns, the instruments punctuating the rhythmic, deep-pitched rising of the chanting voices.

After a short time the monks rose, donned hats which resembled feathered yellow crescents—the hats signify their membership in the sect called Gelupa, "the Virtuous Order of the Yellow Hat"—and began a procession out of the temple. The purpose of this Tag Juma ceremony was to purify the area of negative spirits. As the monks filed out, we saw that, in addition to the instruments, some carried what appeared to be ornately filigreed, three-foot-tall, pyramid-shaped, red wax totems, topped by white skulls. The monks descended the stairs on either side of the temple entrance and assembled in the courtyard below. Soon, the Head Abbot appeared and, with a bell in one hand and a piece of blue and white silk in the other, accepted a ceremonial goblet from an assistant. All watched intently as a clear liquid was poured into it, and then, after some chanting, the Abbot tossed the liquid onto the ground. This was repeated several times.

Finally, the monks again lined up and this time marched off past the temple, down a gravel path and out into the forest. A short distance away had been prepared what could be loosely described as a teepee made of straw with a large opening in its center. As the monks approached it, they tossed the wax totems into the opening. When all of the totems had been thrown in and a circle of chanting monks surrounded it, a match was lighted and the straw teepee exploded in a blaze of combustion. So much for those evil spirits!

Before leaving, we walked through the adjacent village, collecting a trail of smiling children. It is here, in the workshops of the Handicraft Center, that Tibetan rugmakers, tailors and cobblers craft the distinctive Tibetan-style articles for export around the world.

Because we had stayed on to see the Tag Juma ceremony, we missed the bus which would have connected with our flight to New Delhi. Our alternate plan was to take another bus to Patankote, the halfway point, and then take the overnight train to Delhi, arriving on the morning of the day we were expected.

Sherpa's final kindness was to have the jeep driver take us back to the Guest House to collect our suitcase, and then deposit us at the bus stop down in the village of Dharamsala.

As we reflected on the day and all the generosity extended to us, we realized that perhaps we should have tried to overcome the sense of respect and deference which kept us from requesting an audience with the Dalai Lama on such short notice. Later, while reading of the informality and ease with which His Holiness has welcomed other Westerners, we promised ourselves to one day try to thank him personally. But, we had received the answer to our question, seen the treasures of the Tibetan Library, been privileged to witness and film a seldom-seen ceremony by the Lamas; the purpose of our brief visit had been accomplished.

So far in our journey we had visited the accessible areas of India described by the legend of Saint Issa as well as the major spiritual centers of the country's history. We had been exposed to Jains, Hindus, Sikhs, and Buddhists, both the people and their ideas. I should note that Islam, although a major force in modern India, was not founded until the 7th Century A.D. and did not figure in the travels of Saint Issa so it was not a part of our search.

Pausing to look back on the past weeks and the relative ease with which we had been able to accomplish our goals, an inescapable conclusion was growing within us, we were being blessed in our efforts. A path seemed almost to have been cleared before us by a grace filled hand. We met no objections, we received support everywhere, even from the weather.

Now we were about to take a detour from the legend. During the course of the research we had been surprised to discover the apostle Thomas had traveled to India after the death of his master, had preached for fifteen years and then been martyred there. Our next stop was the city of Madras on the eastern coast of south India, the location of Thomas' grave and the apostolic cathedral dedicated to his memory.

Bronze Buddha in the Library of Tibetan Works and Archives, Dharamsala.

Chapter XIII

DOUBTING THOMAS IN INDIA

The first Biblical references to the apostle Thomas are found in Matthew, Mark and Luke. The book of John refers to "Thomas who is called Didymus (twin)."

Thomas was present when the news reached Jesus of the death of Lazarus. Later, when Jesus tells of his decision to go back to Judea at the request of Lazarus' sisters, even though there would be danger, Thomas says, "Let us go too, and be killed along with him."

At the Last Supper when Jesus told the disciples that he would soon leave them, Thomas spoke, "Lord, we do not know where Thou art going; how are we to know the way there?" Jesus replied with an answer which has illuminated the spiritual path for Christians ever since, "I am the Way; and the Truth, and the Life; no one comes to the Father, but by me. If you had known me, you would have known my Father also; henceforth you know him and have seen him."

The origin of the phrase "doubting Thomas" is known from the incident after the resurrection.

Now Thomas, one of the twelve, called the Twin, was not with them when Jesus came. So the other disciples told him, "We have seen the Lord." But he said to them, "Unless I see in his hand the print of the nails, and place my finger in the mark of the nails and place my hand in his side, I will not believe."

Eight days later, his disciples were again in the house, and Thomas was with them. The doors were shut, but Jesus came and stood among them, and said, "Peace be with you." Then he said to Thomas, "Put your finger here, and see my hands; and put out your hand, and place it in my side; do not be faithless, but believing." Thomas answered him, "My Lord and my God." Jesus said to him, "Have you believed because you have seen me? Blessed are those who have not seen and yet believe."[1]

In that moment Thomas represented the many to come, especially in our 20th Century, who would require experience before believing in things divine. Even though Thomas had been present at the raising of Lazarus and other of Jesus' miracles, he again needed to see for himself. And Jesus satisfied his need.

The final instructions from Jesus to his disciples is found in Matthew:

Now the eleven disciples went to Galilee, to the mountain to which Jesus had directed them. And when they saw him they worshipped him; but some doubted. And Jesus came and said to them, "All authority in heaven and on earth has been given to me. Go therefore and make disciples of all nations, baptizing them in the name of the Father, and of the Son and of the Holy Spirit, teaching them to observe all that I have commanded you; and lo, I am with you always, to the close of the age."[2]

And so the disciples were commissioned as missionaries. From observers and followers together under the leadership of their master to solitary ambassadors carrying the word of what they had seen and heard into a world unknown to them.

But did Thomas really go to India?

One of the earliest writings to refer to Thomas as the apostle who evangelized in India is a Syrian work from the 2nd Century entitled "The Doctrine of the Apostles." One passage says:

> After the death of the Apostles, there were Guides and Rulers in the Churches; and whatever the Apostles communicated to them, and they had received from them, they taught to the multitudes. They, again, at their deaths also committed and delivered to their disciples after them everything which they had received from the Apostles; also what James had written from Jerusalem and Simon from the City of Rome, and John from Ephesus and Mark from the great Alexandria, and Andrew from Phrygia and Luke from Macedonia and Thomas from India, that the epistles of an Apostle might be received and read in the churches in every place.[3]

Another passage says:

> India and all its own countries and those bordering on it even to the farthest sea, received the Apostles' Hand of Priesthood from Thomas, who was Guide and Ruler in the Church which he built there and ministered there.[4]

A second source of early information is the work entitled, "The Acts of St. Thomas," believed to date from the early 3rd Century.

> When the Apostles had been for a time in Jerusalem, they divided the countries among them in order that each one might preach in the region which fell to him; and India fell to the lot of Thomas.[5]

Another passage gives Thomas' reaction to the news of his mission, "I am a Hebrew; how can I teach the Indians?" Later, in the same narrative, he says stubbornly, "Whithersoever Thou wilt, O Lord, send me; only to India I will not go. . . ."[6]

In spite of this stubbornness and doubt, such familiar human qualities, it appears Thomas did go to India. The Roman Catholic Church now regards the Cathedral of St. Thomas at Mylapore as a Basilica because it stands over the tomb of the Apostle.

According to the apocryphal Acts of Thomas, he entered India as a carpenter, preached the Gospel, performed many miracles and died a martyr's death. These writings speak of his travels in the northwest area of India and his conversion of a king named Gundaphar. For centuries this king was considered only legendary. However, in the 19th Century, a large number of coins were discovered in Afghanistan, near the capital of Kabul, and in the western and southern regions of the Indian Punjab. These coins bear the name Gondophares and have been dated between 20 and 45 A.D., the time when Thomas would have been in India.

After some years in the north, Thomas seems to have traveled south along the coast of the Arabian Sea. In the southern state of Kerala where Christians say they have always called themselves "St. Thomas' Christians," there is a strong belief that St. Thomas founded seven churches. These were at Cranganore, Palur, Kottakavu, Kokkamangalam, Niram, Chayal and Quilon. Quilon, still a sizeable town, is one of the most ancient Episcopal Sees in India, created by Pope John XXII in 1330. A church built by St. Thomas in Quilon is believed to have existed for more than a thousand years before being swept away by the sea.

After living and preaching in the communities on the West Coast, Thomas traveled East, reaching the Mylapore coast on the Bay of Bengal. This area was now interesting to us because of the three places sacred to the memory of the

Apostle, Little Mount, where he is said to have sought refuge from pursuers, St. Thomas Mount, where he was captured and killed as he knelt in prayer, and the Cathedral of St. Thomas, which was built over his tomb.

Up until the 17th Century the area had been occupied by Syrians, Armenians, Portuguese, Dutch and French adventurers. The city of Madras was founded by the East India Company in 1639 as its first important British settlement. In 1687 King James II gave the Company the right to establish civil government in Madras with employees and municipal salaries. Today, it is a sprawling collection of colonial administrative centers in huge buildings, contrasted with narrow winding streets filled with shops and houses with sloping bamboo roofs, which have grown up around them. Madras is the political, artistic and intellectual center of South India.

It was raining as we landed. Our bags seemed to have gotten heavier, and the cartilage in our shoulder sockets had just about given out. We gave the taxi driver the name of the Woodlands Hotel and hoped we could get a room without a prior reservation. The Woodlands belongs to a chain of hotels and had been recommended by Indian friends. It is especially known for its food—wonderful tropical fruits and an endless variety of vegetarian dishes, most of which soar off the top of my tolerance scale for peppers and chilis.

We were given a suite with a spacious sitting room, perfect for entertaining friends to tea, a bedroom and a large bath. As I recall, all for the price of thirty-five rupees, about $5.00. We settled ourselves, had lunch and then went out in search of Saint Thomas.

The place called Little Mount is really a little mount, hardly distinguishable from the suburbs around it on the outskirts of the city.

In the course of his travels Thomas arrived here and soon became a favorite of the local king. But the king's ministers and priests opposed him and one day in their sovereign's absence they threatened Thomas' life and forced him to seek refuge in a cave on top of a nearby hillock.

At present, the top of the hill is covered by a small circular church; the amount of land did not allow for the more traditional style, and this church is situated over the cave where Thomas hid.

We walked up the broad steps past the church and proceeded to a tiny building with an arched doorway and wooden doors which covers the entrance. A crevice about five feet by two feet, with several crude steps, led down to a chamber sixteen feet long, fifteen feet wide and seven feet high.

Tradition says Thomas was followed into the cave and then escaped miraculously through a very small opening at the northern end. Miraculous also is the handprint impressed in the granite, said to have occurred as he was clambering out. At the far end of the cave stands an altar where Mass has been offered for centuries.

After escaping from the cave on Little Mount, evidently Thomas thought he had foiled his pursuers and felt safe enough to return to the place about two miles away where he often spent time in prayer. Now called Saint Thomas Mount, it is three hundred feet above sea level, with a steep eastern side and a western slope covering an area of more than seventy-five acres. Its granite hillside is barren except for a few trees surrounding a cemetery of plain white crosses at the bottom of the hill and a cluster of low buildings at the top.

It is not known how long Thomas remained here in prayer, but the traditional story says that, as he knelt before a stone cross he had carved by hand from a boulder, an assassin sent by the ministers of the king crept up from behind and pierced him with a lance. Thomas fell on the stone cross, embracing it, his blood staining the stone and the earth around it.

The stone cross was rediscovered by the Portuguese on March 22, 1547, during excavations for the foundation of the present church. One Francis Govuea described the stone as "well-carved . . . and a bird touching with its beak the top of the cross. He went on to say, "There was found under the stone much earth bedewed with blood as if it were freshly shed, a good portion of it being attached to the stone itself."

There are reports of miraculous "bleeding" of this stone from 1551 to 1704. One such account reads:

> In the year 1558, on the day of the feast, Expectation of Our Lady, December 18th, when the singing of the Gospel of the Mass was started, the stone of the cross began to turn black in color and to distill water in such large quantity, that those who so willed, soaked their linen and rosaries in it. This time, the miracle lasted for four continual hours; when it came to an end, the stone turned to a very white and resplendent color, which fact gladdened all present; and drying itself slowly, the stone lost the bright color and turned to its natural color.[7]

In 1561, the Portuguese, anxious to know the meaning of the inscription on the stone, invited the most reputed Brahman scholar of the day to decipher the writing. It was translated as follows:

> That at the time of the Sagamo Law, Thomas, a man of God, was sent by the Son of God (whose disciple he was) to these parts to bring the people of this nation to the knowledge of God, that he had built there a temple and done miracles; and that finally he was praying on his knees before that Cross he had been run through with a lance by a Brahmin and that the Cross was tinged with the blood of the Saint in His everlasting memory.[8]

The day of our visit the stone was grey, with no sign of a brighter color. The modest stucco church stood on the rocky hilltop, old and alone, with the forbearance of one who had been rooted to one spot while suspecting that somewhere, on another side of the world, the message it, too, carried had gained power, riches and glory almost beyond imagining, and had affected history and the lives of millions.

After finding him dead, the followers of Saint Thomas carried his body to the place six miles away called Beth Thuma, now known as San Thome' de Meliapor, to the church Thomas had built, and buried him there. The place of his burial is now the site of the Cathedral of Saint Thomas, Mylapore.

Our taxi pulled into the churchyard where the boys were playing kickball, and when we asked where we would find the priest, they led us to the small building behind the church where we met Father A. J. Adaikalam, the Vicar-General of the Archdiocese of Madras/Mylapore. A genial, portly man wearing a long white cassock, he was clearly proud of the cathedral and invited us to join him for a tour. Except for the fact that the exterior was painted white, it was a faithful attempt to carry the Gothic tradition. The inside was adorned with beautiful stained-glass windows, marble floors, and beneath the central altar was a statue of the patron saint and a sign reading "The Tomb of Saint Thomas."

We returned to Father Adaikalam's office behind the cathedral, where he apologized for his lack of proficiency in English, which turned out to be perfectly adequate, and proceeded to tell the story.

Father Adaikalam:
Actually, Thomas, according to tradition, arrived in India in the year 52 A.D. He was first in Kerala, on the west coastal side, where he established seven churches. They are still in existence and are renowned for their faith and community. After working there for a couple of years he crossed over to South Tamil, Tamil Nadu, where he is supposed to have stayed and preached all over. His residence was in Little Mount,

between Thomas Mount and Saint Thom, say about five or six kilometers from here.

There he lived and preached, that was his head-quarters. The place of his activity was in Mylapore because this place is rich in Hindu culture and heritage, so he used to come here and live and preach. And he used to go up to the mountain which is called by his name today, Saint Thomas Mount, which is near the airport, where he used to spend nights in prayer, as his master did.

It was on one such time that he is supposed to have been killed and his body is supposed to have been buried in this Saint Thomas Cathedral. This cathedral actually stands over his tomb. Right from the early centuries somehow this tomb had been kept in veneration by the people of the soil. Even at the time of the Portuguese, when this was a fortress, we have got the flagmast still here near the seashore, somehow this particular tomb was always kept intact, although all the other places were under the govern-ment and ruling forces of that time. Even when the Moslems took over this place a Moslem guard was keeping watch over this tomb.

This cathedral was only built in 1886. Formerly there was a smaller church, still earlier there was only the tomb here. That is how this locality has this magnificent cathedral.

Dick:
So, the power of Saint Thomas' vibration has sustained throughout the two thousand years and is still felt strongly?

Father Adaikalam:
Yes. The Christians in Kerala call themselves Thomas Christians, that is a definite thing. There had

been formerly some doubts but there has been made a thorough search and we have got ample proofs from the writings of the Church, from history.

Dick:
There is no doubt now?

Father Adaikalam:
No doubt now. We had the centenary celebrations in 1972; the Holy Father Pope could not be called again because he had come for the Eucharistic Congress in 1965, and we didn't want to trouble him, but he sent his representative, Cardinal Conway, the Primate of Ireland, who presided over the centenary celebration.

Dick:
Was it usual for people to be able to travel to India in the days of St. Thomas?

Father Adaikalam:
In those days most of the traveling was done either by walking or by vehicles that were at that time available. And I think they have traveled by sea to a certain extent. It's a long journey, tedious journey, and hard journey. Even lately, in the time of Saint Francis Xavier, who was our second apostle to India; he traversed the whole of this area by walking and by traveling by ordinary vehicles. There were no cars or planes in those days.

Dick:
Do you know about the possibility that Jesus came to India?

Father Adaikalam:
What we have so far understood is that it is only

a supposition; they have no historic proof to say that
Jesus ever came to India. The reason they might think
this is because Jesus is an Easterner, no doubt, and all
the ways and means of his teachings have an Eastern
trend.

Dick:

We recently met the Shankaracharya from Puri
who made an interesting statement. He said that prior
to Buddhism there was no proselytising or conversion
in religious experience, that Vedanta in the form of
Hinduism was not a converting experience, and that
the Buddha came and then Buddhism became a
religion of conversion. He said it might very well have
been possible that Jesus made contact with that
tradition and then initiated the idea of conversion.

Father Adaikalam:

I have no belief in this statement for this reason.
You see, the Indian religions were not bound by any
uniform tenets. Hinduism is a way of life and Vedantism is an aspiration of the soul to God, men aspiring
to know something about God, that is, the actual
yearning of any individual soul in the world, so
Vedantism is only trying to aspire to reach the
supreme being. Whereas the philosophy of South
India has more philosophical discretions and precepts,
and more concrete ideas. It is something like our
Aristotelian philosophy of the Greeks. Naturally,
Aristotelian philosophy was easily connected with
Christian philosophy and theology. Similarly, the
South Indian philosophy found it easy to come over
to the Christian tenets, easy because after all what is
religion, it is the soul aspiring towards its creator. So
Jesus Christ when he had revealed himself as the Son
of God and could give us the summit of revelation,

and then connect mankind to God by calling Him father, no more thinking of God as something far away being, but closely connected as the son to the father, that is the greatest revelation man had ever. The knowledge that we get through Jesus Christ is appealing to every human being. As Jesus said, he came to preach the gospel to the poor and even today the poorest section of the people easily grasp it, and the simple of heart, humble of heart, immediately grasp it. That is what I understand.

Dick:
    Yes, he was one of them and lived as they did.

Father Adaikalam:
    Yes, as a matter of fact, all religions, we see that they are all trying to give the best of good things to mankind, and somehow give the knowledge of God to man. Every religion tries to do that, and Christianity has this singular privilege, having a person who is not an ordinary man, but a god in man, which is a hypostatic union, as we call it, where the divine nature and human nature are mingled together. Naturally, it is a singular privilege of Jesus Christ, I should say.
    Whereas all the other big personalities that we have come across in the world, founders of religions, or mahatmas, every one of them had their own human cleverness or their sanctity, whereas Jesus could speak of himself with authority as a divine person. That is the only difference that I could say.

Father Adaikalam's certainty about the singular nature of Jesus, that Jesus is the only "divine person" ever to have lived is not surprising until one considers the Avatars, the divine incarnations, which populate the history of his homeland. Because of this history Jesus is revered in India as divine, a reverence not only undiminished but enhanced by the belief that God has appeared in human form before, and since, to give His message to mankind.

It is understandable that the disciples of Jesus, inasmuch as they were provincial fishermen and tax collectors, could have been unaware of these eastern traditions, but one wonders whether they were totally unaware of the Messiah who had lived in their own country less than 100 years before, the Essene Teacher of Righteousness described in the Dead Sea Scrolls who, like Jesus, preached love of one's neighbor, penitence, poverty, humility and chastity. Who, like Jesus, advocated baptism, communion and the observance of the Law of Moses as fulfilled by his own revelations; who was the object of hostility, was condemned and put to death, and whose followers awaited his triumphant return. One wonders if the disciples recognized the similarities between the teachings of Jesus and those of the neighboring Essene community which stored its documents in clay pots inside caves near the Dead Sea.

Two thousand years later, in 1946 to be exact, a young Bedouin named Muhammed the Wolf, was chasing a stray goat when he came upon a cave with the clay pots containing the Essene Manual of Discipline, the War of the Sons of Light with the Sons of Darkness, the Habukkuk Commentary, and the Zadokite Fragments, all of which pre-date the birth of Jesus and indicate the teachings we call Christianity existed as the teachings of a Jewish sect in the century before the man lived whom we call Christ.

We will never know exactly what Jesus' disciples knew, but with our knowledge of the history of avatars in the East and the Essene Teacher of Righteousness, we, at least, have a broader perspective from which to view the life of Jesus. For many, the position that Jesus was the only "Son of God," or "divine person" as Father Adaikalam stated is, in effect, a limiting of the power of God, a shackling of divinity to one physical form for all eternity, and the difficulty in accepting this belief has sent many searching for a more reasonable explanation.

The question is not whether Jesus was divine, but whether or not he is the only person throughout the ages of humanity to be so.

The Cathedral of Saint Thomas of Madras/Mylapore. The diocese was created by Pope Paul V in 1606.

Chapter XIV

I AND MY FATHER ARE ONE

From the Cathedral of St. Thomas our destination was a small village in South Central India called Puttaparthi, and someone who dwells in realms of consciousness beyond our ordinary experience, someone who could tell us more about Saint Issa. Although articles in the London Times have described him as "the most impressive Holy Man in centuries," his practice of discouraging publicity, and the fact that he has not traveled to the west have, for the most part, kept Bhagavan Sri Sathya Sai Baba out of the glare of public attention.

We had been to visit him three times before. Our experience told us the seemingly fantastic stories about Sathya Sai Baba, his omniscience, and his miraculous powers to manifest and heal were really true. We had been in Baba's presence for days and weeks on end. Our astonishment at the manifestations and healings was gradually tempered and we found ourselves left with a desire to comprehend the more profound aspects of the experience and then apply them to our lives. After all, Sai Baba had repeatedly said the miracles are only his calling cards, used to gain our attention so we will take note of what he is telling us about our nature as human beings.

Eight months before setting out on our present trip we

had sent a message to Baba asking if Jesus had, indeed, traveled to India. The response was relayed by friends who were present and took notes as he spoke. They reported Baba said Jesus arrived in India at about age 16. His mother, Mary, had sold household possessions to help him in his journey. He said Jesus was practically penniless in his travels, often having only one meal a day. He wore a loin cloth of the type seen in India today called a dhoti, much like the one depicted in paintings of the crucifixion. According to Baba, Jesus attained Christ consciousness at the age of 25 while in India. Thereafter, he returned to Palestine through Tibet, Afganistan, Persia and areas we now know as Russia.

We were once again on our way to Puttaparthi, this time with the hope Sai Baba would speak to us directly about the missing years. When he did his words corroborated the path the legend says Issa took. Then Baba said,

At all times Jesus Christ had a mind which was pure and which was unwavering and selfless. All the work he did was dedicated to the good of the world. In the early days he used to proclaim himself as the messenger of God and would say he had come to serve all the peoples of the world.

While calling himself the messenger of God he conducted himself as the servant of the people and for twelve years he was often found in meditation. As a result of his meditation he proclaimed himself as the son of God. He was moving closer to God.

He spent five years in the Himalayan regions of India. After coming to India and practicing spiritual disciplines he proclaimed, "I and my father are one."

After experiencing this identity with the father, and proclaiming himself one, identical with the father, he returned to his own country.

The legend of Saint Issa says:

Issa . . . whom the Creator had selected to recall to the worship of the true God, men sunk in sin . . . was twenty-nine years old when he arrived in the land of Israel.[1]

The Bible tells nothing about Jesus' life from the time he was 12 in the temple until he appeared to John the Baptist by the river Jordan. Those 18 years being dismissed with one sentence in Luke 2:52, "And Jesus increased in wisdom and in stature, and in favor with God and man."

According to the Bible, Jesus was about 30 when he appeared to John by the river Jordan in the fifteenth year of the reign of Tiberius Caesar, while Pontius Pilate was governor of Judea and Herod was tetrarch of Galilee.

Now they had been sent (priests and Levites) from the Pharisees. They asked him (John), "Then why are you baptizing, if you are neither the Christ, nor Elijah, nor the prophet?" John answered them, "I baptize with water; but among you stands one whom you do not know, even he who comes after me, the thong of whose sandal I am not worthy to untie." This took place in Bethany beyond the Jordan, where John was baptizing.

The next day he saw Jesus coming toward him, and said, "Behold, the Lamb of God, who takes away the sin of the world! This is he of whom I said, "After me comes a man who ranks before me, for he was before me. I myself did not know him: but for this I came baptizing with water, that he might be revealed to Israel." And John bore witness, "I saw the spirit descend as a dove from heaven, and it remained on him. I myself did not know him; but he who sent me to baptize with water said to me, He on whom you see the Spirit descend and remain, this is he who baptizes with the Holy Spirit. And I have seen and have borne witness that this is the Son of God."[2]

Because of early experiences in church and Sunday school I find it difficult even now to interrupt the scriptures with questions, but isn't it strange that John should twice say about Jesus, "I myself did not know him."

In Luke 1:36 the angel Gabriel said to the young Mary,

> "And behold, your kinswoman Elizabeth in her old age has also conceived a son; and this is the sixth month with her who was called barren. For with God nothing will be impossible." And Mary said, "Behold I am the handmaid of the Lord; let it be to me according to your word." And the angel departed from her.[3]

The son born to Elizabeth, kinswoman of Mary who became the mother of Jesus, was John. Isn't it strange that Jesus and John, generally believed to have been cousins only months apart in age, would not recognize one another unless Jesus had been away from his homeland and the two had not met since childhood.

Upon his return to Palestine Issa would have found it occupied by Romans and divided into five provinces ruled by the three surviving sons of Herod the Great. Roman garrisons and fortresses lined the Eastern border while additional strongholds held strategic spots throughout the country. All this was supported by heavy taxes levied on the income and property of each household in the land.

Twenty-four Jewish sects quarreled with one another but, with the exception of certain of the aristocracy, they united in opposition to the Roman practice of inundating their country with philosophy, customs, architecture and religious practices adopted from pagan Greece.

The provinces of Galilee, Judea and Perea, were mostly rural. The majority of Jews lived in villages of several hundred inhabitants scattered throughout the countryside. They worked at their trades, tended their flocks and farmed the dry land, seldom venturing more than one day's journey from home. They lived in mud brick houses clustered on hillsides with narrow unpaved streets and dusty alleys winding toward a central square where women drew water from a communal well and shopped in an open air market as old men sat passing the time of day. Children were schooled in the synagogue, boys learning ancient Hebrew from which their everyday language of Aramaic had derived. Larger towns had scribes as teachers and religious advisors to interpret the laws of the scriptures.

Life was hard, work punctuated by a weekly Sabbath day of rest and yearly religious feasts and festivals such as Passover, and the one day when the name of the Lord could be spoken, if only by the high priest, the day of repentance for the sins of the nation, the Day of Atonement.

A second point of unity among the differing sects was a fervid anticipation of freedom in a world to come which would be delivered to them alone by their long awaited Messiah.

The legend tells us . . .

IX

1. *Issa . . . whom the Creator had selected to recall to the worship of the true God, men sunk in sin . . . was twenty-nine years old when he arrived in the land of Israel.*

2. *Since the departure therefrom of Issa, the Pagans had caused the Israelites to endure more atrocious sufferings than before, and they were filled with despair.*

4. But Issa, notwithstanding their unhappy condition, exhorted his countrymen not to despair, because the day of their redemption from the yoke of sin was near, and he himself, by his example, confirmed their faith in the God of their fathers.

10. The Israelites came in multitudes to listen to Issa's words; and they asked him where they should thank their Heavenly Father, since their enemies had demolished their temples and robbed them of their sacred vessels.

11. Issa told them that God cared not for temples erected by human hands, but that human hearts were the true temples of God.

12. "Enter into your temple, into your heart; illuminate it with good thoughts, with patience and the unshakable faith which you owe to your Father."

X

1. Issa went from one city to another, strengthening by the word of God the courage of the Israelites, who were near to succumbing under their weight of woe, and thousands of the people followed him to hear his teachings.

2. But the chiefs of the cities were afraid of him and they informed the principal governor, residing in Jerusalem, that a man called Issa had arrived in the country, who by his sermons had arrayed the people against the authorities, and that multitudes, listening assiduously to him, neglected their labor; and, they added, he said that in a short time they would be free of their invaded rulers.

3. Then Pilate, the Governor of Jerusalem, gave orders that they should lay hold of the preacher Issa

and bring him before the judges. In order, however, not to excite the anger of the populace, Pilate directed that he should be judged by the priests and scribes, the Hebrew elders, in their temple.

4. *Meanwhile, Issa continuing his preachings, arrived at Jerusalem, and the people, who already knew his fame, having learned of his coming, went out to meet him.*

5. *They greeted him respectfully and opened to him the doors of their temple, to hear from his mouth what he had said in other cities of Israel.*

6. *And Issa said to them: "The human race perishes, because of the lack of faith; for the darkness and the tempest have caused the flock to go astray and they have lost their shepherds.*

7. *"But the tempests do not rage forever and the darkness will not hide the light eternally; soon the sky will become serene, the celestial light will again overspread the earth, and the strayed flock will re-unite around their shepherd.*

8. *"Wander not in the darkness, seeking the way, lest ye fall into the ditch; but gather together, sustain one another, put your faith in your God and wait for the first glimmer of light to re-appear.*

9. *"He who sustains his neighbor, sustains himself; and he who protects his family, protects all his people and his country.*

10. *"For, be assured that the day is near when you will be delivered from the darkness; you will be re-united into one family and your enemy will tremble with fear, he who is ignorant of the favor of the great God."*

11. The priests and the elders who heard him, (Issa) filled with admiration for his language, asked him if it was true that he had sought to raise the people against the authorities of the country, as had been reported to the governor Pilate.

12. "Can one raise against estrayed men, to whom darkness has hidden their road and their door?" answered Issa. "I have but forewarned the unhappy, as I do here in this temple, that they should no longer advance on the dark road, for an abyss opens before their feet.

13. "The power of this earth is not of long duration and is subject to numberless changes. It would be of no avail for a man to rise in revolution against it, for one phase of it always succeeds another, and it is thus that it will go on until the extinction of human life.

14. "But do you not see that the powerful, and the rich, sow among the children of Israel a spirit of rebellion against the eternal power of Heaven?"

15. Then the elders asked him: "Who art thou, and from what country hast thou come to us? We have not formerly heard thee spoken of and do not even know thy name!"

16. "I am an Israelite," answered Issa; "and on the day of my birth have seen the walls of Jerusalem, and have heard the sobs of my brothers reduced to slavery, and the lamentations of my sisters carried away by Pagans;

17. "And my soul was afflicted when I saw that my brethren had forgotten the true God. When a child I left my father's house to go and settle among other people.

18. "But, having heard it said that my brethren suffered even greater miseries now, I have come back to the land of my fathers, to recall my brethren to the faith of their ancestors, which teaches us patience upon earth in order to attain the perfect and supreme bliss above."

19. Then the wise old men put to him again this question: "We are told that thou disownest the laws of Mossa, and that thou teachest the people to forsake the temple of God?"

20. Whereupon Issa said: "One does not demolish that which has been given by our Heavenly Father, and which has been destroyed by sinners. I have but enjoined the people to purify the heart of all stains, for it is the veritable temple of God.

21. "As regards the laws of Mossa, I have endeavored to re-establish them in the hearts of men; and I say unto you that ye ignore their true meaning, for it is not vengeance but pardon which they teach. Their sense has been perverted."

XI

1. When the priests and the elders heard Issa, they decided among themselves not to give judgment against him, for he had done no harm to any one, and, presenting themselves before Pilate—who was made Governor of Jerusalem by the Pagan king of the country of Romeles—they spake to him thus:

2. "We have seen the man whom thou chargest with inciting our people to revolt; we have heard his discourses and know that he is our countryman;

3. "But the chiefs of the cities have made to you false reports, for he is a just man, who teaches the people the word of God. After interrogating him, we have allowed him to go in peace."

4. The governor thereupon became very angry, and sent his disguised spies to keep watch upon Issa and report to the authorities the least word he addressed to the people.

5. In the meantime, the holy Issa continued to visit the neighboring cities and preach the true way of the Lord, enjoining the Hebrews patience and promising them speedy deliverance.

6. And all the time great numbers of the people followed him wherever he went, and many did not leave him at all, but attached themselves to him and served him.

As the legend says Issa wondered for 18 years, so the Gospels tell of Jesus traveling constantly from place to place during his ministry, at the end of which he was arrested and crucified. Church history attributes this act to the Jews; Jewish history tells another.

Jesus took up the life of a teacher, preaching his own gospel. There was nothing different or un-Jewish in his teachings. He was a liberal; he was against all injustice, in the tradition of the Prophets. He taught the observance of the Mosaic law, compassion for the poor, mercy and tolerance.

He spoke in a soft voice and with a loving heart. He was an inspiring teacher who expressed himself in crystal-clear parables. His messages went straight to the hearts of his listeners.

He was an oasis of comfort in a desert of Roman misery. The humble people flocked to him to take solace in his words, to find comfort in his vision, and to take heart in the hope he held out.

Nothing he preached, taught or said was in contradiction to what other Jewish prophets, rabbis, or sects said or taught.

Jesus was not in danger from Jews. He was in danger from the Romans, for it was no longer safe to teach justice in a land ruled by terror. Judea was sitting on a powder keg of an incipient rebellion, and the Roman cure was to seize all suspects and flay them alive or crucify them . . ."[4]

Jesus concluded this period of his ministry with a trip to Jerusalem for Passover. While there he disrupted the long established custom of selling sacrificial doves and pigeons outside the Temple, a custom considered similar to the selling of candles and crosses in churches today. He also objected to the handling of money on Temple grounds, so he smashed the tables of the money lenders who were there converting the currency of foreign pilgrims.

In spite of these actions, imagine someone interrupting Easter services by smashing the candles and crosses offered for sale and spilling all the collection plates, Jesus was not arrested until three days later.

The gospels, written 40 to 90 years after the fact, say Jesus was arrested at night in the garden of Gethsemane by order of the Sanhedrin, the highest court in the land, and then condemned to death by the Sanhedrin for the crime of blasphemy at the palace of the high priest with the aid of witnesses who had been induced to give false testimony. Then, according to this version, Pontius Pilate reluctantly allowed the sentence to be carried out because he was afraid of what the Jewish crowd might do if he did not.

Jewish law of the time allowed no one to be arrested at night. It was illegal to hold court proceedings after sundown on the eve or day of the Sabbath or of a festival. The Sanhedrin could convene only in the Chamber of Hewn Stones, never in the palace of a High Priest or in any other dwelling. The Sanhedrin could not initiate an arrest. No one could be tried before the Sanhedrin unless two witnesses had first sworn out charges against him. There was no prosecuting attorney, so the accusing witnesses had to state the nature of the offense to the court in the presence of the accused, who had the right to call witnesses in his own behalf. The court then examined and cross-examined the accused, the accusers, and the defense witnesses.

The account in the Gospels has been compared to an unlikely twelve hour scenario in which the U.S. Supreme Court has a man arrested at night, finds witnesses during the same night to accuse him of a crime, condemns him to death without a trial and presses for immediate execution.

The Legend of Saint Issa presents its own version of the events.

XIII

1. Thus Saint Issa taught the people of Israel for three years, in every city and every village, on the highways and in the fields, and all he said came to pass.

2. All this time the disguised spies of the governor Pilate observed him closely, but heard nothing to sustain the accusations formerly made against Issa by the chiefs of the cities.

3. But Saint Issa's growing popularity did not allow Pilate to rest. He feared that Issa would be instrumental in bringing about a revolution culminating in his elevation to the sovereignty, and, therefore, ordered the spies to make charges against him.

4.   Then soldiers were sent to arrest him, and they cast him into a subterranean dungeon, where he was subjected to all kinds of tortures, to compel him to accuse himself, so that he might be put to death.

5.   The Saint, thinking only of the perfect bliss of his brethren, endured all those torments with resignation to the will of the Creator.

6.   The servants of Pilate continued to torture him, and he was reduced to a state of extreme weakness; but God was with him and did not permit him to die at their hands.

7.   When the principal priests and wise elders learned of the sufferings which their Saint endured, they went to Pilate, begging him to liberate Issa, so that he might attend the great festival which was near at hand.

8.   But this the governor refused. Then they asked him that Issa should be brought before the elders' council, so that he might be condemned or acquitted, before the festival, and to this Pilate agreed.

9.   On the following day the governor assembled the principal chiefs, priests, elders and judges, for the purpose of judging Issa.

10. The Saint was brought from his prison. They made him sit before the governor, between two robbers, who were to be judged at the same time with Issa, so as to show the people he was not the only one to be condemned.

11. And Pilate, addressing himself to Issa, said, "Is it true, Oh! Man; that thou incitest the populace against the authorities, with the purpose of thyself becoming King of Israel?"

12. Issa replied, "One does not become king by one's own purpose thereto. They have told you an untruth when you were informed that I was inciting the people to revolution. I have only preached of the King of Heaven, and it was Him whom I told the people to worship.

13. "For the sons of Israel have lost their original innocence and unless they return to worship the true God they will be sacrificed and their temple will fall in ruins.

14. "The worldly power upholds order in the land; I told them not to forget this. I said to them, 'Live in conformity with your situation and refrain from disturbing public order;' and, at the same time, I exhorted them to remember that disorder reigned in their own hearts and spirits.

15. "Therefore, the King of Heaven has punished them, and has destroyed their nationality and taken from them their national kings, 'but,' I added, 'if you will be resigned to your fate, as a reward the Kingdom of Heaven will be yours."

16. At this moment the witnesses were introduced; one of whom deposed thus: "Thou hast said to the people that in comparison with the power of the king who would soon liberate the Israelites from the yoke of the heathen, the worldly authorities amounted to nothing."

17. "Blessings upon thee!" said Issa. "For thou hast spoken the truth! The King of Heaven is greater and more powerful than the laws of man and His kingdom surpasses the kingdoms of this earth.

18. "And the time is not far off, when Israel, obedient to the will of God, will throw off its yoke of sin;

for it has been written that a forerunner would appear to announce the deliverance of the people, and that he would re-unite them in one family."

19. Thereupon the governor said to the judges: "Have you heard this? The Israelite Issa acknowledges the crime of which he is accused. Judge him, then, according to your laws and pass upon him condemnation to death."

20. "We cannot condemn him," replied the priests and the ancients. "As thou has heard, he spoke of the King of Heaven, and he has preached nothing which constitutes insubordination against the law."

21. Thereupon the governor called a witness who had been bribed by his master, Pilate, to betray Issa, and this man said to Issa: "Is it not true that thou hast represented thyself as a King of Israel, when thou didst say that He who reigns in Heaven sent thee to prepare His people?"

22. But Issa blessed the man and answered: "Thou wilt find mercy, for what thou has said did not come out from thine own heart." Then, turning to the governor he said: "Why dost thou lower thy dignity and teach thy inferiors to tell falsehood, when, without doing so, it is in thy power to condemn an innocent man?"

23. When Pilate heard his words, he became greatly enraged and ordered that Issa be condemned to death, and that the two robbers should be declared guiltless.

24. The judges, after consulting among themselves, said to Pilate: "We cannot consent to take this great sin upon us, —to condemn an innocent man and liberate malefactors. It would be against our laws.

25. *"Act thyself, then, as thou seest fit." Thereupon the priests and elders walked out, and washed their hands in a sacred vessel, and said: "We are innocent of the blood of this righteous man."*

XIV

1. *By order of the governor, the soldiers seized Issa and the two robbers, and led them to the place of execution, where they were nailed upon the crosses erected for them.*

2. *All day long the bodies of Issa and the two robbers hung upon the crosses, bleeding, guarded by the soldiers. The people stood all around and the relatives of the executed prayed and wept.*

3. *When the sun went down, Issa's tortures ended. He lost consciousness and his soul disengaged itself from the body, to reunite with God.*

4. *Thus ended the terrestrial existence of the reflection of the eternal Spirit under the form of a man who had saved hardened sinners and comforted the afflicted.*

5. *Meanwhile, Pilate was afraid for what he had done, and ordered the body of the Saint to be given to his relatives, who put it in a tomb near to the place of execution. Great numbers of persons came to visit the tomb, and the air was filled with their wailings and lamentations.*

6. *Three days later, the governor sent his soldiers to remove Issa's body and bury it in some other place, for he feared a rebellion among the people.*

7. *The next day, when the people came to the tomb, they found it open and empty, the body of Issa being*

gone. *Thereupon, the rumor spread that the Supreme Judge had sent His angels from Heaven, to remove the mortal remains of the Saint in whom part of the divine Spirit had lived on earth.*

8. *When Pilate learned of this rumor, he grew angry and prohibited, under penalty of death, the naming of Issa, or praying for him to the Lord.*

9. *But the people, nevertheless, continued to weep over Issa's death and to glorify their master; wherefore, many were carried into captivity, subjected to torture and put to death.*

10. *And the disciples of Saint Issa departed from the land of Israel and went in all directions, to the heathen, preaching that they should abandon their gross errors, think of the salvation of their souls and earn the perfect bliss which awaits human beings in the immaterial world, full of glory, where the great Creator abides in all his immaculate and perfect majesty.*

11. *The heathen, their kings, and their warriors, listened to the preachers, abandoned their erroneous beliefs and forsook their priests and their idols, to celebrate the praises of the most wise Creator of the Universe, the King of Kings, whose heart is filled with infinite mercy.*

The final stanzas of the legend raise the question if Jesus' body was, indeed, resurrected, or whether it was moved and re-buried at the order of Pilate. All that can be said with certainty is that the Christian church is based on the belief that Jesus, as the only Son of God, was resurrected by God from the dead. In addition, however, we now know of eastern teaching which acknowledges dematerialization and rematerialization of a body by a Master through the conscious control over the physical body.

Chapter XV

BECOMING THE CHRIST

Home again after our visit to India, questions continued to arise, the answers to which seemed locked in the mysteries of the missing years. The primary one being, was there a connection between the Biblical teachings of Jesus and the teachings he would have encountered on a journey to the East. To answer it, we began by looking at the history of that first century after Jesus' death.

We found that while Thomas was living and preaching in India, his brother disciples were also traveling and dying for their beliefs, Andrew to Greece, Peter to Rome, John to the eastern Mediterranean, Philip and Bartholomew to Greece and Hierapolis and James to Jerusalem.

As the apostles and their followers spread the word, as Paul, after his revelation on the road to Damascus, became no longer a persecutor of Christians but a messenger of the Christ he had never met, Christianity spread into the areas of the world dominated by Rome.

Paul was the most influential because he took the word beyond the Jewish communities to the pagani, pagans, the word then meaning pre-Christian villagers. He was called the apostle to the Gentiles because he carried the word to the Romans, Corinthians, Galatians, Ephesians, Philippians, Colossians and Thessalonians. His subsequent letters to this

131

widespread flock survived to become a major part of the New Testament.

Church historians believe the four gospels we now study were written between 65 A.D. and the end of the 1st Century after Jesus' death. Why a gap of over thirty years from the crucifixion to the recording of it? Perhaps there were documents detailing Jesus' life which did not survive to be discovered or perhaps, as suggested by S. G. F. Brandon of Manchester University in England, the first Christians felt no need to record Jesus' life because he was expected to return at any moment. It is possible that as this first generation began to die out they realized the stories of their master's life and teachings would die with them unless written records were to survive.

Whatever the reason, the oldest copies of the gospels date only from the 3rd Century, so we are faced with a gap of perhaps two hundred years through which it is impossible to trace the progress of the gospels or the accuracy of the words attributed to Jesus. It is not known through whose hands they passed, or which of the over one hundred Christian sects of the time influenced the writings. For Christianity did not spread as a pure form, it was greatly influenced by Judaism in Judea, by Hellenism in Greece, by Gnosticism in Egypt, and by the pagan beliefs of Rome.

The end of the 1st Century saw Christian communities in areas we now know as Jordan, Lebanon, Syria, Turkey, Bulgaria, Greece, Albania, Yugoslavia, Italy, Egypt and Libya. By the end of the 2nd Century Christian colonies had reached into Europe as far north as Germany and as far west as France and Spain. In North Africa they stretched to Tunisia and Algeria, in the east to Iraq and Iran.

In spite of the differences which separated them, the early Christians were united in the belief that Jesus was the son of God who would return one day soon to create the Kingdom of God on earth. They believed that because they were among the true believers, when Judgment Day came, they would be granted eternal life in heaven. They wanted to believe that all men were equal under God, that compassion and dignity were the inheritance of every man, and that there was hope of salvation and everlasting happiness after death.

Jesus' teachings have reached us through the filters of Judaic, Greek, Syrian, Egyptian and Roman societies, and through Gnostic, Hellenistic, Neo-Pythagorean, and other religious and philosophical traditions.

One of the early moves was to separate Christianity from the Judaism of its heritage, to change the perception of God from the Old Testament Yahveh, the God of retribution, to the father of the gentle Christ, the God of Love.

Historians count over one hundred different creeds among the followers of Jesus in the first three centuries. Some sects demanded followers imitate the simple and austere life of Christ, some practiced abstinence from meat, wine and sex, others practiced self-mortification and condemned marriage as a sin. Some taught that Jesus' body was merely a phantom, not human flesh, and others considered him only a man. The Adoptionists and followers of Paul of Samosata thought he had been born a man, but had achieved divinity through moral perfection.

The classical faiths continued to be practiced by the majority, Syrians worshipped their Baals, Egyptians their Gods and despite Emperor Hadrian's destruction of Jerusalem, Judaism survived to preach the Old Testament. But the Romans seemed to suffer a type of gradual exhaustion which led to their political, military, as well as spiritual decline.

Early Christian teachers and writers appeared who viewed Christianity not as a new religion but who believed with Saint Augustine when he said:

> That which is called the Christian religion existed among the ancients, and never did not exist, from the beginning of the human race until Christ came in the

flesh, at which time the true religion which already existed began to be called Christianity.[1]

As an example of this, the concept of the fatherhood of God did not originate with Christ as is generally assumed, for the Aryans of India addressed God as the father, as did the Greeks. And there were other examples.

Jesus taught, "Blessed are the pure in heart for they shall see God."

The Vedas say, "Having realized Him by means of meditation, with a pure mind and sincere heart, the wise will never meet with death."

Jesus taught, "Love thy neighbor as thyself."

The Vedas say, "Thou art That."

Jesus taught, "Do unto others what ye would have others do unto you."

Buddha said, "With pure thoughts and fullness of love I will do toward others what I do for myself."

The most famous Christian of the time was Origen who undertook to demonstrate that all Christian dogmas existed in the writings of the pagan, pre-Christian philosophers. He argued that the scriptures had deeper layers of meaning, spiritual and moral. To Origen, God was not Yahveh, but the first principle of all things. Christ was not the human figure of the New Testament, but the Logos or Reason, created by God and thus subordinate to Him. Origen professed a religion and faith based on reason.

And Plótinus, one of the greatest pagan philosophers, was called a Christian without Christ because his philosophy was accepted so completely by the later followers of Jesus.

Early in the 4th Century, 312 to be exact, a young Roman general was about to come to power. His name was Constantine and the Empire he would inherit was widespread and divided among many beliefs. These differences among religious factions were causing political and military turmoil. He had observed the failure of three campaigns of persecution against Christians and had noted how, although in the minority, these strong people had remained united while the pagans spawned more and greater differences.

Then Constantine had a vision which was pivotal in his life and in the history of Christianity. The afternoon before the famous battle of the Mulvian Bridge, he saw a cross of fire light up the sky and the Greek words, "en toutoi nika," in this sign conquer. That night a dream voice ordered him to have his soldiers mark the symbol of Christ on their shields. He obeyed. The next day, October 27, 312, he outmaneuvered his enemy, forcing the opposing army to fight with its back to the river with no possibility of retreat.

He proceeded to Rome as victor and master of the Western Roman empire? Soon Constantine met with Licinius, ruler of the Eastern empire, and the two proclaimed religious tolerance and restored property to Christians who had been persecuted.

Constantine, nominally aligned with the Christians, and Licinius, defender of the pagans, eyed each other's realms and jockeyed for power until war broke out between them in 323. Constantine emerged the winner, declared himself a Christian and invited his subjects, east and west, to convert.

His actions as a Christian strongly suggest his purpose in converting was more political than spiritual. Although proclaiming himself a Christian, he filled his court with pagan philosophers and scholars, and seldom followed the requirements of his new faith.

But Constantine's support of Christianity gained for him the immediate loyalty of troups faithful to the cause. He was impressed by the order and morality of their conduct, by their obedience and by the fact that they rarely revolted against the state because they had been taught submission to civil power.

Christians had also been taught to believe in the divine right of kings, and since Constantine aspired to become an absolute monarch, the ruler had found his subjects. He also saw in the existing network of priests and bishops the foundation of a strong centralized church bureaucracy which could also function as a political tool. As his power solidified, he favored the church more openly, even to exempting its property from tax laws.

Dissenting factions within the church alarmed him. The most serious heresy arose over the differing opinions as to the nature of Jesus. The primary opponents in the controversy were Arius, an ascetic, and the Bishop Alexander.

Arius' position was that Jesus was begotten of the Father and so could not be "consubstantial" or "co-equal" with Him. Jesus was, rather, the first and highest of all created beings, the Logos. These views were widely held among the clergy.

Bishop Alexander convened a council of Egyptian bishops, reaffirmed the position that Jesus was not only one with the Father but one with the Holy Spirit as well, and proceeded to unfrock Arius and his followers. But the controversy continued.

When Constantine heard of the problem, a division which now threatened the very unity of the church, he wrote letters to Arius and Alexander in which he expressed an astounding lack of comprehension of the problem. He said the differences were "trifling and unworthy of such fierce contests," about a question "in itself entirely devoid of importance."

When his letters had no effect on the situation which was fast becoming vital to the political state of his empire, he convened a council of all the Christian Bishops to be held at Nicaea near his capitol of Nicomedia. Three hundred and eighteen Bishops appeared, mainly from the eastern provinces. Apparently Pope Silvester I as well as the majority of western Bishops did not attend.

Arius affirmed the logic of his position that if Jesus was created by the Father he was subsequent to Him and could not be equal to Him.

An archdeacon named Athanasius argued, "If Christ and

the Holy Spirit were not of one substance with the Father, polytheism would triumph." He conceded the difficulty of picturing three distinct persons in one God, but argued that reason must bow to the mystery of the Trinity.

The concept of the Trinity was endorsed by Constantine, and the new creed, the Nicaean Creed, was written.

> We believe in one God, the Father Almighty, maker of all things visible or invisible, and in one Lord Jesus Christ, the Son of God, begotten . . . not made, being of one essence with the Father . . . who for us men and our salvation came down and was made flesh, was made man, suffered, rose again the third day, ascended into heaven, and comes to judge the quick and the dead . . .[2]

"At Nicaea the majority eventually acquiesced in the ruling of the Alexandrians, yet this result was due, not to internal conviction, but partly to indifference, and partly to the pressure of the imperial will."[3]

Constantine appreciated the threat polytheism could pose to his empire and so he not only made this ruling on the Trinity and the Nicaean Creed, he imposed an Imperial edict ordering all books by Arius be burned, making concealment of such punishable by death. And in 389 A.D., just sixty-four years after the first council at Nicaea, Christian armies put to fire the library of Alexandria which was the greatest known repository of ancient knowledge, forever obscuring the records of the past.

As it became apparent to us that the question of the lost years was central to the entire belief structure of the church, we had to consider the possibility that the official canonized nature of Jesus as perceived and perpetuated by the church had come about as the result of political expediency on the part of an emperor trying to keep his dominions under control.

But what then is the nature of Jesus? Was he born "consubstantial" and "co-equal" with God, as was argued and later enforced by that first council at Nicaea, or did he attain the Christ nature, the Christ consciousness, in the course of his lifetime. Was this attainment signified at that moment described in Luke when, just after being baptized, the Holy Spirit descended upon him in the form of a dove?

The theory that an individual attains divine consciousness as a result of actions in life is at the basis of all Eastern religions and would have been familiar to Saint Issa. Such evolution toward the divine is believed to be the result of many lifetimes of progression through the delusion that man and God are separate, until all the self-erected barriers have fallen, allowing perception of our true nature, the awareness that we are one with God, we are God, to shine through. In this sense each individual completes a trinity with the Father and the Holy Spirit.

Is there a window through time to yesterday, to the past of unwritten history? Is there an imperishable repository for our thoughts, words and actions?

Saints and psychics throughout history have referred to an Akashic (Akash meaning the ether of the universe) record, a universal memory existing somewhere beyond time and space. This record is believed to contain a continuous record of mankind's earthly experience, perhaps comparable to a cosmic computer which only a privileged few have been able to tune in to.

One such man was the world-renowned Edgar Cayce, a 20th Century American prophet who throughout the years demonstrated his ability to read the Akashic record in more than 14,500 clairvoyant readings. His ability to diagnose and cure illnesses, frequently without ever seeing the patients, gave enormous credibility to his work because the cures were verifiable.

Cayce, a devout Christian, was called the sleeping prophet

because the answers came while he was in a sleep-like trance; in fact he had no knowledge of the words he had spoken until the carefully recorded transcripts of the sessions were read back to him upon waking. He explained the source of his information as follows:

> Upon the skein of time and space are the records made. For thoughts and deeds are indeed things, and their currents run with time and space and make their impressions there; just as in the mental forces it is gradually being comprehended that as the man, as the being thinketh in his heart, so is he.[4]

In one such trance state, information was revealed about Jesus' education. Cayce said:

> The period of study was only at the time of his sojourn in the temple, or in Jerusalem during those periods when he was quoted by Luke as being among the rabbis or teachers. His studies in India, Persia and Egypt covered much greater periods that there might be completed the more perfect knowledge of the material related to those cleansings of the body in preparation for strength of the physical as well as in the mental man.[5]

In India we were able to learn of the traditional cleansing practices Cayce spoke about. Cleansing is not only a physical act but a purification of the thoughts, words and actions of the individual. The goal is oneness, the merging of the purified individual with God; it is salvation, union, yoga.

Cleansing of thoughts is attained by focusing the attention on a chosen aspect of God. When, through this practice of concentration, the individual transcends the sense of self and merges with the object of attention, it becomes meditation. The continued practice of meditation and prayer frees the mind of external influences and desires, and allows it to perceive its divine inner nature.

Cleansing the mind permits the body to function free of stress and disease. The body can then manifest its energy in the form of strength, endurance and abilities we call miraculous.

The creative energy of life is symbolically perceived as residing within each individual, coiled as a serpent at the base of the spine from where it will rise and travel along a path, activating seven centers of energy called chakras. These centers represent survival, reproduction, power, universal love, creativity, awareness and finally, self-realization.

The Biblical Jesus exhibited all the results of these practices, the freedom from personal desires, the transcendence of self, endurance, and miraculous abilities culminating in the resurrection of his own body.

In the course of Edgar Cayce's trance readings on the subject of Jesus another revelation appeared.

He came, this soul we know as Jesus, in many different ages, as a spokesman to "manifest the first idea." These incarnations were given as Adam, Enoch, Melchizedek, Joseph, Joshua, Jeshua, and finally Jesus.[6]

Cayce further said:

This soul who came as Jesus has come in all ages when it has been necessary for the understanding to be centered in new application of the same thought: "God is spirit, and seeks such to worship Him in spirit and in truth."[7]

The implication here being the soul of Jesus appeared throughout time in different bodies and carried different names. This led us to the question of reincarnation.

During our search for the answers to these questions, we talked to Swami Kriyananda, an American-born disciple of

Paramahansa Yogananda, the founder of the Ananda Community and Meditation Retreat in Northern California.

Paramahansa Yogananda is known as the founder of the Self-Realization Fellowship and as the author of "Autobiography of a Yogi," a classic book which has opened the door for decades of searchers to a deeper understanding of Eastern thought and its compatibility with the teachings of the West.

Yogananda spent thirty years in Southern California, dedicating himself to explaining and expounding the teachings of the Old and the New Testaments. He is also known for the miraculous event that occurred after his death, miraculous in the respect that his body, which was interred at Forest Lawn Cemetery in Glendale, California, showed no signs of physical deterioration for over twenty days.

Swami Kriyananda has devoted his adult life to sharing Yogananda's vision of the supportive cooperative community as the most effective way for society to sustain itself in the future. The Ananda Cooperative Village, a self-sustaining farm with a thriving publishing and printing facility, is the result of Yogananda's vision and of Kriyananda's dedication to his master's ideal.

When we asked Kriyananda about any knowledge he might have regarding the lost years, he began by quoting from one of his teacher's discourses that had been recently published. Yogananda had said:

God made Jesus Christ an Oriental in order to bring East and West together. Christ came to awaken the divine consciousness of brotherhood in the East and the West. It is true that Christ lived in India during most of the eighteen unaccounted-for years of his life, studying with India's great masters. That doesn't take away from His divinity and uniqueness. It shows the unity and brotherhood of all saints and avatars.[8]

Kriyananda then went on to say:

Yogananda was talking not from a level of schol-
arship but of intuition. His vision of Christ may or
may not be true in the minds of the reader, not
knowing who Yogananda was or not knowing well
enough how authentic his words were. An interesting
story might help to substantiate their belief.

In the early years of his mission here in America
he used to say that Jesus sent him to the West to
bring back original Christianity. One time in Boston
he received an anonymous letter from someone,
saying he was wrong in sponsoring Jesus Christ in this
country. Yogananda wanted to know who this person
was and prayed to be shown.

About a week later he was in the Boston public
library where he saw a man sitting on a bench under
a window. He went over and sat next to the man and
said, "Why did you write me that letter?" The man
was very astonished and said, "What do you mean,
what letter?" Yogananda said, "The one in which you
said I was wrong in calling Jesus Christ the son of
God, and the letter in which you said it was a myth."
The man practically jumped up off his seat and
demanded, "How did you know, how did you know
I wrote that letter?" "Well," said Yogananda, "Never
mind, I have my ways." "But," he added, "I wanted
you to know that the power that enabled me to find
you enables me also to know that Jesus did live and
that he was what the Bible claims he was."

So the point is that Yogananda had the power to
know that Jesus lived, he had the power to know
Jesus' life and he was speaking from a level, not of
opinion, but of inner vision.

It actually makes sense, too, if we look at it from
a standpoint of logic. If the disciples had really been
writing his story as it's presented in the Bible, they
would have said something, they would have at least
said Jesus grew up and worked in his father's shop, or

they would have said he went off to the wilderness to pray. The fact that you find absolutely no reference at all in the Bible from the age of twelve to the age of thirty indicates that someone took those years out but didn't dare manufacture information to substitute.

In fact, one gets the impression that other things were taken out of the Bible, too. You know, the early Christians used to believe in reincarnation, the Jews believed in it, the orthodox Jews still believe in it. And Origen, one of the greatest theologians, second to Saint Augustine even, so great was he, said that he got the teaching of reincarnation from apostolic times. This teaching wasn't taken out of Christian doctrine until 553 A.D. at the Second Council of Constantinople. They found recently that Pope Vigilius who was present in Constantinople, boycotted that council. I think there was only one prelate from Rome. They banned Origen for political reasons and, at the same time, took out all his teachings, including that of reincarnation. But we do find little glimpses and hints in the Bible about reincarnation, about Elijah, for example, coming before the Messiah. Jesus saying that John the Baptist was Elias or Elijah. Many other passages are indicative of this teaching being accepted. For example, when Jesus said, "Whom do men say that I am," the disciples said, "Some say Jeremiah, or one of the other prophets." Jesus didn't correct them for saying that people were saying he was an incarnation, which is obviously what was meant, or one of the ancient prophets.

So we get the impression that the Bible was tampered with for the usual reason, which is institutional religion. When they try to institutionalize religion they also bring out the more convenient things that will support their church dogmas, and this is what I think they must have done, and what Yogananda indicated that they did do with the Bible. That there were many high and deep teachings there that are not available except through the lives of great saints who lived those teachings and realized them in their own lives.

If, in fact, reincarnation was a part of the early teachings of the church, it would have been in harmony with the teachings of other philosophers of the time and with the great historic religions of the East studied by Saint Issa. Reincarnation was a fundamental concept of the Egyptian mystery schools, both Hermetic and Gnostic, of Persian Mithraism, of Alexandrian Neoplatonic theology and of the Jewish Kabalists. The Magi, disciples of Zarathustra in Persia, three of whom were the first men to be aware of and honor the birth of Jesus, considered it the first of their teachings.

These schools taught the immortality of the soul and the transience of the body. They called it variously metempsychosis, pre-existence of souls, transmigration of souls, or reincarnation.

Is the principle of reincarnation found in the Bible? In the book of Proverbs, King Solomon says:

> The Lord possessed me in the beginning of his way, before his words of old. I was set up from everlasting, from the beginning, or ever the earth was.[9]

And what about the New Testament?

> And as they were coming down the mountain, Jesus commanded them, "Tell no one the vision until the Son of man is raised from the dead." And the disciples asked him, "Then why do the scribes say that first Elijah must come?" He replied, "Elijah does come, and he is to restore all things; but I tell you that Elijah has already come, and they did not know him, but did to him whatever they pleased. So also the Son of man will suffer at their hands." Then the

disciples understood that he was speaking to them of John the Baptist.[10]

Now Herod the tetrarch heard of all that was done, and he was perplexed, because it was said by some that John had been raised from the dead, by some that Elijah has appeared, and by others that one of the old prophets had risen.[11]

Then said the Jews unto him; Thou are not yet fifty years old, and has thou seen Abraham? Jesus said unto them, "Verily, verily, I say unto you, before Abraham was, I am."[12]

Jesus began to say unto the multitudes concerning John . . . "This is he, of whom it is written, Behold I send my messenger before thy face, which shall prepare thy way before thee. Verily I say unto you, among them that are born of women there hath not risen a greater than John the Baptist . . . and if ye will receive it, this is Elias, which was for to come, He that hath ears to hear, let him hear."[13]

Jesus speaking of John:

This was he of whom I spake, He that cometh after me is preferred before me; for he was before me.[14]

To take a reasoned approach to reincarnation, we need to understand cause and effect, the law of Karma.

For a time after my own first attempts to grasp it, I was confused because I had heard people say it was fatalistic to believe in karma; if we did believe it meant our lives were preordained by fate and we had surrendered control of our destiny. They insisted all the poverty in Asia was caused because people felt what happened to them was their fate and could not be changed or improved upon.

I finally came to see how the principles of karma and free will interact.

It's true that through the cause and effect of karma we create conditions we will have to face in the future. It is also true, however, that when those conditions appear we have free will to control our reactions to them. We can react out of impulse or we can react consciously knowing that this new action, too, will return to us.

We then progress from a state of automatic unthinking reaction, through thoughtful considered reactions, to the point where all action is done with a consciousness of personal detachment and, ultimately, surrender to God. We no longer react or act out of self-interest but out of surrender to the will of God.

This is called "burning the seeds of karma," and through this, one is released from the imprisonment of life after life in a physical body to return to the limitless universe of love that is God.

The New Testament also contains examples which can be seen as referring to cause and effect.

For truly I say to you, till heaven and earth pass away, not an iota, not a dot, will pass from the law until all is accomplished.[15]

You have heard that it was said to the men of old, "You shall not kill; and whoever kills shall be liable to judgment." But I say to you that everyone who is angry with his brother shall be liable to judgment; whoever insults his brother shall be liable to the council, and whoever says, "You fool!" shall be liable to the hell or fire.[16]

For if you forgive men their trespasses, your heavenly Father also will forgive you, but if you do

not forgive men their trespasses, neither will your
Father forgive your trespasses.[17]

Judge not, that you be not judged. For with the
judgment you pronounce you will be judged, and the
measure you give will be the measure you get.[18]

So whatever you wish that men would do to you,
do so to them, for this is the law and the prophets.[19]

Jesus is speaking to the paralytic who had been
brought to him, "My son, your sins are forgiven."
Now some of the scribes were sitting there, questioning in their hearts, "Why does this man speak thus? It
is blasphemy! Who can forgive sins but God alone?"
And immediately Jesus, perceiving in his spirit that
they thus questioned within themselves, said to them,
"Why do you question thus in your hearts? Which is
easier, to say to the paralytic, "Your sins are forgiven," or to say, "Rise, take up your pallet and
walk?" But that you may know that the Son of man
has authority on earth to forgive sins, he said to the
paralytic, "I say to you, rise, take up your pallet and
go home."[20]

Here Jesus seems to be saying that the paralysis was
caused by the sins and when the sins were forgiven by the
Lord the paralysis was cured.

If we accept the principles of reincarnation and karma,
we can then look upon the life of Jesus with new comprehension. We can understand Edgar Cayce when he said:

Jesus is the man, the activity, the mind, the
relationships that He bore to others. Yes, He was
mindful of friends, He was sociable, He was lonely,
He was kind, He was gentle. He grew faint, He grew
weak, and yet gained that strength that He has
promised in becoming the Christ, by fulfilling and
overcoming the world!

Ye are made strong in body, in mind, in soul and purpose by that power in Christ. The POWER is in the Christ. The PATTERN is in Jesus.[21]

This pattern of evolution through reincarnation of the soul in successive lifetimes is the classic pathway to divine consciousness as revealed by God to the ancient rishis and passed through time by the science of yoga and the philosophy of Vedanta.

If we accept this principle we can see that Jesus' missing years could have been spent in becoming in Christ, in cleansing, purifying and evolving, in tapping the creative energy of life residing in the chakras until he came to the realization that goes beyond the mind to permeate every part of the conscious and subconscious being, the realization that "I and my Father are One."[22]

Chapter XVI

SIGNS AND WONDERS

Saint Issa was taught to . . .

cure physical ills by means of prayer, to teach and to expound the sacred scriptures, to drive out evil desires from man and make him again in the likeness of God.[1]

Jesus said, "Except ye see signs and wonders ye will not believe."[2] And, in the course of his ministry he subdued the elements, manifested objects, healed the sick and raised the dead.

A miracle is defined as "an event that appears unexplainable by the laws of nature and so is held to be supernatural or an act of God,"[3] yet the history of science is a chronicle of man's growing awareness of the laws of nature. The miracles of yesterday are taken for granted today.

Ancient yogis delved into the mysteries of the universe by sharpening their sense of inner awareness. Today scientists work externally, their senses extended by instruments and tools. The greatest discoveries, however, continue to be influenced by flashes of insight and intuition such as the thought experiments of 26 year old Albert Einstein which produced the theory of relativity, the scientific recognition of the interchangeable nature of matter and energy.

While the intention of modern science is to conquer the external world, yogis approached the external through the internal, starting with the phenomena at hand, the human body, mind and spirit. Their observations of cause and effect developed acute sensitivity. This heightened sensitivity revealed that the core of human existence, the only change-less aspect of a human being, was the soul, the part of an individual that is one with God, that is God. By understanding the body and mind as subordinate to the soul they learned that lasting peace and satisfaction were not attainable from the ever-changing outer world. From this followed self-sufficiency, allowing them to be independent. No one object in the world had more value or desirability than any other, so the world could be viewed with detachment, objectivity and, ultimately, freedom. The physical world became a platform for the aspiration to bliss filled worlds of spirit.

The law of nature was revealed as a continuum; begin-ningless, yet first discerned in realms of the most subtle spirit, where all is but the divine elemental consciousness of creation, long before the journey into denser domains of matter where western thought was later to divide it into ever-warring opposites of man and nature, thought and emotion, good and evil. All nature was seen as part of the continuum of consciousness and, therefore, was knowable through consciousness.

The difference between science today and that of the ancient yogis is that the yogis experienced the vast external as a macrocosm reflecting in mirror image the smallest particle of creation. They knew, as did Emerson who wrote,

The universe is represented in every one of its par-ticles. Everything is made of one hidden stuff. The world globes itself in a drop of dew . . . The true doctrine of omnipresence is that God appears with all His parts in every moss and cobweb."[4]

I and my Father are One.[5]

The miracles of Jesus and Saint Issa may seem inexplicable, they are, however, part of the science of yoga which Swami Chidananda explained to us in Rishikesh as . . .

". . . the result of yogic powers that accrue to a master yogi, an adept in yoga who has ascended the highest stage and so these powers are called siddhis and they comprise powers by which one has control over internal as well as external nature. One has control over the elements, and one has control of life and death, as it were, and what seems impossible is possible to such a master."

There are two sets of circumstances under which miracles have been observed. First, the power described by Swami Chidananda which accrues to one who has ascended the highest stage, in direct proportion to the discipline and self-mastery attained by that individual. These disciplines can be described as the means by which an individual brings under his own control his body, mind and senses in order to clear them from the path so that the power which is latent within him and, in fact, within each of us, can meet and link with the universal divine omnipotence. As a result of this linking the individual has brief and limited access to that power.

Once a certain amount of power has accrued the individual is faced with the responsibility of deciding how to use it. It can be used and demonstrated or it can be internalized to propel the individual to greater spiritual awareness. Once expended however, it is gone, and additional power only comes through additional discipline.

This lengthy process of earning and expending siddhi powers, while going on today, is far less observable than in the past. Warnings against demonstration of these hard earned siddhis make the point that the very pride and ego gratification an aspirant is struggling to overcome are the all but inevitable results of exhibiting these powers in the world. That is why they are so seldom seen.

And Jesus said, "Who was it that touched me? . . .
Someone touched me; for I perceive that power has
gone forth from me."[6]

The second type of power has rarely been possessed. At
times throughout history men have observed and recorded
the actions of figures so much larger than life, so far beyond
limited human comprehension that the earliest have come to
be categorized as mythological and the more recent have
been doubted and denied.

These beings exhibited powers at will, without the
running down of the battery effect that controls the actions
of those with siddhi powers. These phenomena are described
in the scripture of Vedanta as God's grace, His response to
the prayers of mankind for help in righting the conditions of
the world, for restoring the balance of righteousness.

They are called Avatars, either full or partial, depending
on the number of powers they manifest, powers which are
dictated by the needs of mankind at the time, they are used
solely for the benefit of mankind. Because he and his father
are truly one, an Avatar is in complete accord with his body,
mind and all the elements of nature which are, after all, God
also in other less fully manifested forms. It may appear from
our point of view that an Avatar is in control of these
elements, that he is bending the universe to his independent
will. Contrasted with our own lack of control in the universe,
this is a very impressive idea. Actually, there is no separation
between the will of the infinite God and His finite manifestation. The Avatar is divine purpose in human form.

In the lands through which Issa journeyed the human
body, as with all matter, was perceived as a form of
consciousness, and as such could be affected, positively or
negatively, by consciousness. Simply expressed, it was, and is,
mind over matter. The transformation or movement of
particles of matter/energy/consciousness was possible, and it

was possible to withdraw the breath of life from a body and then return it through a process known as samadhi.

Through the disciplines of purification the life force, called the kundalini, rises through the seven chakras to the highest chakra called the Sahasrara.

> When the Kundalini rises to the Sahasrara and the mind goes into samadhi, the aspirant loses all consciousness of the body. He loses knowledge of the outer world. He does not see the manifold any more. His reasoning comes to a stop. The individual soul and the supreme soul become one.[7]

The body may appear lifeless during this time, and it is said that after 21 days the tenuous connection between soul and body begins to fade and the soul seldom chooses to return.

In the case of Jesus his crucified body appeared to be lifeless from sunset on Friday evening when the Roman soldier pierced it with his spear in order to demonstrate he was, in fact, dead, until sometime before sunrise on Sunday, about 36 hours. It is this return to life, this resurrection that even more than the other miracles unifies Jesus, son of Joseph and Mary, with Issa, student of the ways of the ancients. And, as if planned by Jesus/Issa to be revealed only at a time when the complementary nature of east and west could begin to be understood, tangible material evidence has appeared to support the supposition that the knowledge gained by Issa was demonstrated by Jesus, thus making it possible to reconcile the two young men in the minds of the world and to restore the unity of their experience and teachings.

After describing events of Jesus' crucifixion, the Gospel of St. Luke goes on to say . . .

> Now there was a man named Joseph from the Jewish town of Arimathea. This man went to Pilate

and asked for the body of Jesus. Then he took it down and wrapped it in a linen shroud, and laid him in a rock-hewn tomb, where no one had ever yet been laid.

It was the day of preparation, and the sabbath was beginning. The women who had come with him from Galilee followed, and saw the tomb, and how this body was laid, then they returned, and prepared spices and ointments.

On the Sabbath they rested according to the commandment.

But on the first day of the week, at early dawn, they went to the tomb, taking the spices which they had prepared. And they found the stone rolled away from the tomb. But when they went in they did not find the body.[8]

In the excitement and wonder that followed as they ran to look for their risen savior, something was left behind, the shroud which had covered the body while it lay in the tomb. Today, almost two thousand years later, it is believed by Popes and scientists that the shroud which covered the body of Jesus not only has survived but has preserved for us an accurate image of the physical likeness of Jesus.

The Holy Shroud of Turin is a piece of white linen cloth approximately 14 feet 3 inches long and 3½ feet wide. What distinguishes it from any similar piece of cloth and establishes it as one of the most mysterious aspects of the life of Jesus is the fact that the fabric contains faint markings of unkown origin as well as blood stains. The markings picture a face and body while the blood stains demarcate lacerations caused by a crown of thorns, wounds inflicted by nails through the wrists and ankles, as well as a spear which pierced the heart. Together the markings and the blood stains present an image of suffering and death the world has known about for over 1900 years but never expected to see.

The first historical reference to the shroud is found in the Gospels. Little is known of its whereabouts during the early centuries. This was a time of persecution of Christians so it is understandable that such a precious relic would have been kept safely hidden away. At some point it was moved from Jerusalem to Constantinople where records indicate it was seen in 436 A.D. when the Empress Pulcharia, a granddaughter of Emperor Constantine, built the Basilica of Saint Mary to house the shroud and to display it to the public every Friday. The shroud was again reported seen in Constantinople in 1150 A.D. and later in 1201 A.D. In 1204 Constantinople was sacked by Crusaders and the shroud taken as part of the spoils of war. It is believed to have been carried north to Vienna and then west to France. About 150 years later, in 1355, it was displayed to the public in Lirey, France.

In 1389, a controversy arose in which it was charged that the image had been painted on the shroud. Many believed the charge at that time, however scientific investigation later proved it was impossible for the marks on the fabric to have been caused by any form of paint or pigment.

In 1452 it was taken to Chambery in Southern France and presented to the Duke of Savoy, a member of the powerful family which would later come to rule all of Italy. At Chambery the shroud was kept folded in a silver chest. On the night of December 3, 1532, a fire engulfed the palace and the silver chest began to melt and drops of molten silver fell onto the folded cloth, burning a pattern of holes in the shroud. As it was pulled from the fire water further stained the fabric.

Carmelite nuns repaired the holes with fresh altar linen and lined the shroud with white velvet. They also marveled at the fact that although marks damaged both sides of the shroud, the image of the body was left untouched.

In 1578 the owners of the shroud had become the Royal Family of Italy and they arranged to move this most precious relic across the Alps to a new cathedral in Turin, the capitol of their realm. The Cathedral of Turin with the Chapel of the Holy Shroud was built near the end of the 15th Century. It is adorned with two domes, the lower above the main altar while a second rises 200 feet above the Chapel of the Holy Shroud. Because of the danger of fire which had threatened the shroud the chapel and altar were built entirely of black marble. Here the shroud is rolled around a cylinder which is sealed before being placed in the silver reliquary which is then put inside a heavy iron box and placed behind a double iron grillwork. With the exception of the years during World War II when it was moved to Southern Italy for safety, the shroud has remained in Turin.

The shroud was first photographed in 1898 by Secundo Pia. The image itself is an imprint from the body and as such is reversed and serves as a photographic negative. Because of this phenomenon, Pia was first to see the correct likeness of the figure, the first to see the photograph of the man believed to be Jesus.

The event attracted the attention of the French Academy of Sciences in Paris. The speculation was that this was the "world's oldest photograph," and certainly worthy of scientific study. The examination was undertaken by a senior member of the Academy, Dr. De Lage. Preliminary studies were focused on the authenticity of the shroud as shown by evidence carried on the fabric itself, and upon the phenomena that it might possibly be the "world's oldest photograph." In 1902 De Lage presented the findings to a packed meeting of the prestigious French Academy of Sciences. His evidence for authenticity was sound and was not challenged. Thirty years later Pope Pius XI who was a scientist as well as Pope, said:

We speak now as a scientist, not as Pope. We have personally investigated the Shroud and we are convinced of its authenticity.[9]

Since the Middle Ages Popes have spoken of the shroud. Pope Paul VI called it "the most important relic in the history of Christianity,"[10] and Pope John XXIII said, "This can only be the Lord's doing!"[11]

Many questions about the shroud are now being answered with scientific techniques of the 20th Century. One of the first invariably raised is whether or not a skillful artist in the 14th Century could have painted the image. Studies of this question have brought three conclusions.

First, the fabric of the shroud is woven linen in a 3 to 1 twill weave, with a herringbone pattern throughout. This type of weave has been found in fabrics from the Middle East which have been dated from 100 to 300 A.D., and this weave was unknown in France in the 14th Century.

Secondly, art historians point to the fact that the style of art of the 14th Century was so different from the realism and anatomical precision portrayed on the shroud that it is inconceivable it was produced at that time. The conclusive finding on this theory is that there is no evidence of paint, brush strokes or pigment of any kind on the fabric itself.

Dr. Max Frei, a noted Swiss criminologist, has scientifically "time-dated" the cloth in an unusual way. Authorities have so far been unwilling to cut the cloth to provide samples for Carbon 14 dating, so Dr. Frei took pollen scrapings from the shroud and subjected them to criminological analysis. These tests revealed the presence of pollen fossils that could only have come from plants that grew exclusively in Palestine at the time of Jesus. He also found pollen samples that help to trace the travels of the shroud. This is based on the presence of pollen fossils which date from the time of the crusades and came from areas of Turkey. Still other fossils date from France of the Middle Ages.

The major unresolved question is, just how was the delicately detailed image of the body formed on the cloth?

In the early 1900's, biologist Dr. Paul Vigon and physicist Rene Colson developed the "vaporgraph" theory. They speculated that the perspiration from the body had reacted with the spices packed around it to form a gas which then rose and stained the cloth. The gas would have had to travel in a perfectly straight line, both up and down. While experiments have succeeded in staining fabric, the kind of precise detail of the shroud was never recreated.

Another popular theory involved heat radiating from the body and "scorching" an image on the cloth. This heat is thought to have occurred during the miraculous conditions of the resurrection, when the body dissolved in a "blaze of light."

Some experiments were carried out in England, but so far attempts to produce a similarly detailed image have failed. The closest known approximations to the shroud images were discovered by a Dr. Volkringer at the French Academy of Sciences. He found that leaves accidentally left between the pages of a book for over one hundred years had formed a highly detailed negative image on the paper several pages away. From this it was postulated that some form of life energy had radiated from the leaves, through the adjoining pages, and formed the image.

By extending this line of reasoning it has been postulated that similar life force energy radiated to form the image on the shroud, the difference being that the leaves radiated at a low intensity for a hundred years while the body of the man on the shroud radiated at a very high intensity for some period of time during the hours Jesus lay in the tomb.

The recent discovery of Kirlian photography, the ability to photograph energy flares given off by living things, human as well as plant and animal life, has added weight to this theory. It has even been found that an aura of energy, perceived as light when photographed, remains when a portion of a leaf has been cut away. All this had led to speculation that the energy flares we see via Kirlian photography may be related to the phenomenon of halos or auras.

Christian saints and angels, as well as Jesus himself, have traditionally been portrayed with a golden circle of light around the head. Is it possible these halos represent an unseen aura projected by the godly, an emanation once seen by men and portrayed in art that is too subtle for our eyes?

What the Bible calls "the single eye," and Eastern philosophy calls "the third eye," enables some individuals to perceive the auras of people around them. What they reportedly see is that the aura of light around an ordinary man extends some two or three feet from the body, while the aura of a saint extends twenty or thirty feet, giving it an intensity at the body surface of over ten times that of a man whose consciousness is blocked by ego, illness, and other human limitations.

If we believe Jesus' consciousness was free of limitations, either because he had cleansed his mind, mastered his body and released the life force of his chakras, or if we believe Jesus was free of human limitations because he was the Son of God, it follows in either case that radiation intensity from his body could have been very great. For some, this theory goes a long way toward explaining the body images left on the burial shroud. It also explains why no other shroud images have been found in the centuries following the death of Jesus.

Scientists are continuing the search for a definitive explanation of the markings on the shroud. They have established to their satisfaction what the shroud is not; it is not a painting or a modern fabrication. But they cannot tell us what it is.

The face on the Holy Shroud of Turin. Left, the image as it appears on the Shroud, a photographic negative image. Right, the positive image. The cover painting by artist Larry Smith is based on this image.

Chapter XVII

FINDING THE GOAL OF LIFE

Saint Issa's middle years fit into the context of Jesus' life with fulfilling symmetry. They bring us closer to solving the question of the missing years and connect us to our spiritual lineage as well. How often have we heard that east and west would never meet, but they do in Jesus/Issa, not only meet but merge.

It now seems almost as though the Biblical omission was part of a design by which Jesus left us with a mystery, a mystery intriguing enough to entice our 20th Century minds through the looking glass of our own reflection into a realm where we could begin to see the promise of ourselves as inseparable parts of a divine whole. No longer sinners born outside the pale, struggling to enter, but loved children separated from God only by our chosen pre-occupation with the temporary, impermanent things around us.

The past few decades have seen a visible increase in the number of westerners, young and old, trying to understand who they are and where they come from as young Issa did, people who chose to put away the books and philosophy of others to look for truth directly. Like Issa, a great number of them turned eastward in their search. In my case it began at age 26. I could look back on an uneventful childhood growing up in Southern California with palm trees, smog and

A-bomb drills between classes. I had earned a B.A. in Music from the University of California at Santa Barbara and had just returned from 2½ years of living and working in Europe.

It was in Europe that I first began to see patterns, those of others but especially my own, stretching with dulling repetition out into the future. Once I had seen them I needed to find out what they were, these reactions and feelings which ran my life. I wanted to know where they came from and how I could re-order them.

Back home in California I started to work as a secretary in a record company and moved into a small house off a secluded dirt road in Laurel Canyon, barely 7 minutes from the Sunset Strip. In the late 1960's "the canyon" was a vortex of energies . . . writers, actors, but especially musicians spreading their visions to the rest of the country and the world. The energy was raw and forceful, often enhanced by drugs as it swirled and collided through those hills. Many tried to spread their vision by lighting fires, figuratively and literally, and found themselves suddenly burned out.

I had a brief interlude of experimentation with drugs which left me with a feeling of uneasiness. Somewhere inside I seemed to know that artificial methods were superficial, that the only significant change would have to come from inside, from confronting, understanding and disciplining the person I found there.

I began to meditate and read Eastern philosophy, particularly Vedanta, and found in the principles of karma and reincarnation a logic and balance which satisfied my need to start understanding myself and the world around me. After 16 months I grew restless in my job and when an opportunity appeared for transfer to a division where I would be working more closely with music and musicians, I took it. I had heard some interesting things about the man who would be my boss, Richard Bock. I knew he founded Pacific Jazz and World Pacific Records in the early 50's, and after selling them to Liberty/United Artists had remained on to head his division. He had produced such artists as Ravi Shankar, the Jazz Crusaders, Les McCann, Gerry Mulligan, Chet Baker, Jean-Luc Ponty and George Duke, among others. I soon found out he was separated and had a 3½ year old son named Ronnie whom he was crazy about. We had met briefly when I first came to work and, with the exception of one casual lunch with others from the office when we talked briefly about philosophy, our only contact in the subsequent year and a half had been in the office or recording studio.

I was surprised when I received a call from him the Friday before I was to begin the new job inviting me to a yoga class Monday after work. The teacher, Ivan Markoff, lived simply, supporting himself by the earnings of his yoga classes and spending the rest of his time writing and meditating. Dick had known Ivan for years and we soon began to spend more and more time with him.

One Sunday Ivan mentioned a manuscript he was writing. He explained he had read the biography of a spiritual teacher in India who had manifested extraordinary abilities since birth, someone whose consciousness was unimpeded by time and space, who knew the past, present and future, and who seemed to effect beneficial changes in the consciousness and everyday lives of people who came to him, either physically or through prayer and meditation. Ivan had been having powerful experiences of this person in his meditation and had been inspired to write an article combining the biographical information with his personal experiences of Bhagavan Sri Sathya Sai Baba.

A short time later Ivan called to say someone would soon be speaking at the East-West Cultural Center who had just seen Sathya Sai Baba in India. The speaker, another old friend of Dick's named Indra Devi, had just come from her second visit to Sai Baba and spoke in glowing terms of her experiences. She had some Indian films showing a small man standing in the distance before a large crowd. He wore a deep orange robe which hung straight from his shoulders to the ground, his skin appeared dark in the sharp contrast of the harsh Indian sunlight, and his hair was full and dark around his head. She showed us a rosary of large white pearls and a ring which appeared as a diamond or white sapphire and said that Sai Baba had materialized them out of the air before her eyes.

Finally, she explained that Sathya Sai Baba was believed to be the reincarnation of a saint who had lived in Western India named Sai Baba of Shirdi. When Sai Baba of Shirdi was dying in 1918 he told his followers he would be reborn in 8 years. Eight years later, in 1926, hundreds of miles away in a tiny village in South India, Sathya Sai Baba was born.

Someone in the audience asked if books were available on Sai Baba. She replied that books were not available in this country, in fact the only English edition book on Sai Baba of Shirdi had been out of print for years.

Somehow the reading and meditation I had been doing must have prepared a place in my mind which could accept as possible these things which were clearly out of the ordinary, things which seemed to belong more to Biblical times than the second half of the 20th Century. I had no books, no photographs, only a captivating awareness that on the other side of the earth someone lived who appeared to be the embodiment of the spiritual principles which had appealed so strongly to my mind and heart.

Three days later I made a chance visit to the Vedanta Bookstore in Hollywood. I was in the shop only a few moments when a clerk approached and asked if he could help me. My first response was to say no, I was just browsing. Then something jogged my memory and I asked if they had a book about Sai Baba of Shirdi. He said he knew the book I was looking for but that it had been out of print and unavailable for some years. I turned away and he went back to his counter.

Seconds later I heard him calling to me in a soft voice. He had just slid open a cabinet door and was pointing to the edge of the top shelf where a lone copy of a book sat with a red dust jacket. As I approached he handed it to me. The title was "The Incredible Sai Baba" by Arthur Osborne. That title perfectly expressed our feelings in that moment, our surprise at finding a ten-year-old edition of an apparently unavailable book. The clerk started to apologize by saying he was sure it had not been there before, he couldn't imagine where it had come from, etc. I just smiled and hurriedly paid for it. I was surprised and excited, but after the stories I had just heard this experience was not totally unbelievable. After all, the Bhagavad Gita says, "When the disciple is ready the teacher appears."

Soon afterwards Dick went to London to record Buddy Rich and was hit by a heart attack. Throughout the experience he felt himself calling out to Baba, so when he survived with no damage to his heart he made up his mind to go to India as soon as he could. His health was strained by the travel, but he reached the ashram in good spirits just days before the yearly festival celebrating Sai Baba's birthday.

Sai Baba usually suspends his practice of granting personal interviews immediately prior to a festival but continues to give darshan. Darshan is a Sanskrit word meaning to have sight of, and at Prasanthi Nilayam Baba emerges twice daily from the Mandir or prayer hall to walk among the people seated outside, women on one side, men on the other, who have been waiting for him to appear. He accepts letters, blesses religious articles, occasionally speaks a word or two, and if one watches carefully it is occasionally possible to observe the gentle circular motion of his right hand which precedes the manifestation of vibuthi, sacred ash. The vibuthi is symbolic of the ultimate reality of all matter, and of the reality which remains when the dross of the ego is burnt away by the fire of illumination. It is a symbol of detachment, and is taken for physical, mental, emotional and spiritual healing.

On the surface darshan might appear to be a cursory routine, but this impression disappears in the experience. His presence has the power to affect everyone present in a seemingly infinite variety of ways. A glance, an expression, perhaps a word which might appear casual to an observer somehow penetrates deep inside to answer, console, inspire and convey joy of a unique nature. Baba is like the lens through which the light of the sun is gathered and directed onto bits of straw to start a fire which provides heat and light, or the solar energy cell capturing the rays of the sun and converting them to a form of energy we can use to light our consciousnesses.

Dick was to stay five days and, in spite of the crowds, have two interviews. Coming face to face with someone about whom countless miraculous stories have been told, someone who has for over thirty years manifested powers far above the realm we call human, does not often happen in life. Add to this conditions such as jet lag, a recent heart attack, a not quite final divorce, plus the heat and strange food of a foreign country and one wonders what he could have been feeling or have expected to encounter.

Dick still doesn't speak much about what Baba said to him that day in 1968. He did tell us later about two materializations which took place. The first occurred when Sai Baba held his hands up as if to receive something. The next instant a small brass urn about three inches high appeared in the empty air between and slightly above his hands and dropped lightly into them. Sai Baba emptied the urn onto some paper by turning it over and urging the vibuthi out with his forefinger. As he continued it became apparent the growing pile was much larger than could normally have fit into it.

The room where they sat is quite small, probably 12 x 14 feet and next to it is a stairway which leads to the same sized room above which is the extent of Baba's private quarters. Baba began to speak to Dick about his past, his recent illness and his work. At the conclusion of their talk Baba materialized a ring, quite large, and I might add, a perfect fit, with an enamel image of himself seated in a ceremonial chair, right hand upraised in blessing. The enamel was framed in what appeared to be a silver mounting 3/4 of an inch wide and 1-1/8 inches long. Over the enamel was a thin clear lucite-like shield to protect the image.

The interview concluded and as the group left the room someone noticed the ring Baba had just materialized for Dick was itself materializing vibuthi. From the upturned hand on the enamel image a clearly visible trickle of grey ash had formed and was collecting along the edges. Word quickly spread about the on-going miracle and Dick was besieged by those wanting to see it. The phenomenon of the vibuthi ring lasted throughout the following day when Baba again called Dick for an interview. This time he spoke about Dick's future and assured him he was aware of his struggle to find the spiritual meaning of his life.

The following morning Dick left for home and I was waiting when he arrived. He was wan and exhausted, but there was something else that was different. He was tired but happy, still weakened from the heart attack but alight with some inner joy I had never seen in him before. And it did not disappear even when Air France announced that his luggage with all the tapes and film of his trip had been lost, temporarily they hoped.

Luckily, two of his gifts for me were in his pocket. The first was prasad, blessed food, which Baba had distributed personally on his birthday. When Dick received two he decided the extra one was meant for me. This Indian sweet, touched by Baba's own hands, sat for months on my meditation table until I realized the intangible links to him were stronger than any tangible signs and I ate it with pleasure. The second gift was a small circular medallion with Baba's picture that Dick had bought in the village outside the ashram. The airline was right, the luggage showed up 6 days later.

During the next 14 months life went on with added purpose. People who saw Dick's home movies of the trip told others who also wanted to see them. In May of 1969 World Pacific Records released an album entitled "Sathya Sai Baba Chants the Bhajans."

I had not been to India nor had I physically met Baba, yet he had come to represent a powerful presence for me. The words "God is everywhere" of Sunday school days had taken on real meaning and I began to view things about me as all having divine consciousness on a relative scale from inert stone, through animate beings on up into the realm of boundless consciousness where beings such as Sai Baba reside and from where they view all souls as embodiments of the divine. Of course this was only an intellectual perception, but with grace it may one day be all-pervasive.

Dick's recording schedule returned to its pre-heart attack intensity, his divorce became final and to celebrate we took his son with us to Woodstock where Dick recorded Ravi Shankar's famous performance in the rain at that historic event.

All year long whenever the question of returning to India arose Dick had said we would both go in early 1970. When it became clear he could not get away, I decided to borrow the money, take a leave of absence from work, and make the trip alone.

By the time I boarded the plane that February morning in 1970 almost two years had passed since I first heard of Sai Baba. Much of that time had been spent trying to comprehend the meaning of his presence and why, when I had never been particularly religious or philosophical, I should have become so enthralled at this stage of life. After all, I was 28, college educated, self-supporting and single. Dick and I had skirted the topic of marriage every time it came up. The pain of the recent divorce, his second, had convinced him he didn't want to go through that again. My feelings were ambivalent.

It was the concepts of karma and reincarnation, the logic of cause and effect, followed by personal responsibility which captured me. It revealed the source of those behavior patterns I had observed and made clear the unanswered questions about the inequities of circumstances which had been glossed over in church sermons on the mysterious ways of God. I never had believed He was playing a cosmic game of hide-and-seek. The odds were just not fair.

I now understood that mental and emotional patterns were the result of past actions, and the only way to keep them from goose-stepping repetitiously off into the future was to interrupt the rhythm, sneak in there between cause-effect, cause-effect, or cause-effect, effect, effect, and reorder the sequence. I began to see that untangling the web I had spun for myself was now a function of perception, of recognition that each thought, word and act takes off with a pre-paid return ticket, and that such awareness must ultimately be applied to every aspect of conscious and unconscious thought and action. But where did I go for the strength to begin this process?

After 30 hours in the air my flight reached Bombay where I was greeted by Lakshmi Shankar and her sister Kamala Chakravarty. I had met them while they were staying in Los Angeles, so this was a lovely reunion. After a few hours sleep Kamala hired a taxi to show me the city. At one point we passed a small temple with lines of people standing outside. She explained this was a temple to Lord Ganesha and that day, Tuesday, was the most auspicious day to visit, hence the crowds stretching for blocks in either direction. I told her I would like to see the temple because Ganesha was one Hindu deity I had come to know something about. I had learned this aspect of God with the body of a man and the head of an elephant was prayed to for help in overcoming obstacles.

It seems because the elephant has his instrument of action, his trunk, in the middle of his forehead between the eyes, he is always conscious of and concentrating on his actions, which is the secret to overcoming obstacles and succeeding in new endeavors. How simple, especially when contrasted with our tendency to do several things at once while paying close attention to none of them. Kamala suggested we visit the temple on my way back from the ashram on a day when we would not have to wait hours to get in.

The next morning I took an early flight to Bangalore and engaged a taxi for the final 3 hour ride to Sai Baba's ashram. The ride was hot but uneventful. The highway was not crowded and I could see why, under every piece of shade someone was resting, some of the larger trees were surrounded by whole herds of goats or black water buffalo.

After some time we passed out of Mysore state, since renamed Karnataka, into the state of Andhra Pradesh, and after 2½ hours traveling straight north we made a sharp right turn and started east. Now the road was worn and as it passed through tiny villages I could see in through open doors where women were hunched over one-burner kerosene stoves, cooking the ever-present rice for the midday meal. Men were standing or squatting in the shade, young girls were walking back from the village well, having drawn up water from below the moss-covered surface and filled the five-gallon clay jugs they carried on their heads. The younger children played chase with each other, or chickens or baby goats, but rarely with dogs. Dogs eat too much and are too expensive to keep as pets.

After winding through several such villages and passing numerous soggy rice fields we rounded a curve, drove through a gate and stopped. We had reached the back entrance to the ashram.

It was 3:00 P.M. when the driver deposited me inside the gate. All appeared quiet, few people were stirring. Now that I was there I didn't quite know what to do so I asked where I could find Mr. Kasturi. I had heard his voice translating Baba's speech on the tapes Dick brought home and had read his biography of Baba so thoroughly, I felt I knew him. I was told I could find him in the Post Office at the end of a row of buildings on my right.

Walking along that path was an experience to savor. On my left was the familiar shape of the prayer hall I had seen so often in Dick's film. In front of it was the circle with the standing symbol of the lotus, and underfoot was the warm sandy soil which also seemed like an old friend.

As I approached the whitewashed porch and stepped inside the room which served as the Post Office for the ashram, the whole scene took on an air of Somerset Maugham's tropics. Here was the rough wooden desk with antique black phone, the heat and slowly whirring fan, the stacks of letters on coarse paper with foreign-looking stamps and two or three big flies circling like drones waiting for instructions from ground control. Mr. Kasturi was seated at the desk, his head resting on crossed arms and, like everyone else at this hot time of day, he was fast asleep. Someone came in and started to wake him, but I asked them not to. I was still bouncing inside from the long car ride and welcomed a moment of quiet.

Shortly the phone rang and Mr. Kasturi answered it. We smiled at each other while he carried on a conversation in Telegu, the local language. When he hung up I introduced myself. To my everlasting surprise, he stood up quite matter-of-factly, and, as though it were a matter of importance, said, "Oh, I must go tell Baba you've come." Still smiling, he walked out of the room.*

Forty-five minutes later I was sitting on the ground with perhaps 200 other women in front of the mandir or prayer hall waiting for my first sight, my first darshan of Baba. For the first time in my life I knew I was exactly where I should be.

Mr. Kasturi had returned to the Post Office after a few minutes with the key to a room in one of the guest houses behind the prayer hall. Several young boys appeared to help

---

*I found out later a dear friend named Charles Penn, one of the handful of people in the U.S. who had been to Sai Baba at that time, had mentioned my coming in his correspondence with Mr. Kasturi.

carry my luggage and soon I was standing alone in a bare room, my suitcases at my feet, wondering what to do next. Just then a small woman with a smiling face appeared at the doorway. Her name was Jayalakshmi, she supervised the ashram hospital, spoke fluent English and was, I learned later, full of stories about growing up in the same village with Baba. She pointed out the floor-style "facilities," and explained that water would be delivered in clay jugs every morning and the electricity came on for 2 hour periods twice a day.

I wrapped myself in a fresh sari and after a quick lesson from Jayalakshmi on how to get up from a cross-legged sitting position without undressing at the same time, we headed for the front of the prayer hall. She pointed out a spot for me to sit about 30 feet from the door to what she explained was the interview room, and then went off to stand at the back of the crowd. So there I sat, a tall blonde in a sea of small women with long shiny black hair. They were of all ages and scattered throughout the crowd were children ranging from infants to teenagers. A large group of men was seated to our left. Everyone was silent.

Directly in front of me was the central focus of the ashram, the prayer hall, a simple two-story rectangular building of white stucco. On the inside the central two story high portion is taken up by the temple or prayer hall, and at either end were several small rooms on both levels. I knew that the 12' x 14' interview room was on my right and directly above it was the same size room which was the extent of Baba's private quarters. Across the front of the building at the second-story level ran a balcony and below it on the ground floor was an open veranda in the center of which was a two-story portico.

The minutes passed dreamily as I continued to look around, fitting this new reality into the framework of my expectations.

Soon there was a flurry as those around me suddenly adjusted their saris and sat up straighter. Then I saw why.

The door to the interview room had been opened from the inside. All eyes were fixed on that space. Then, slowly, it opened the rest of the way and Baba emerged. There he stood, with the familiar red-orange robe, the full dark hair. He gazed down the length of the veranda, walked slowly to the edge of the step leading to the ground, turned in my direction and looked into my eyes.

At least part of me thought he was looking right at me while another part resisted the urge to look over my shoulder to see who he was really looking at. I watched as he stepped down and walked leisurely along the path cleared by the volunteers, accepting notes, speaking a word now and then, and selecting some for interviews. By the time Baba returned to the veranda over a dozen devotees had been called and were joined by their families to wait at the entrance to the interview room. When the first few had been taken in and Baba was no longer visible the crowd rose and began to walk silently to other parts of the ashram.

Just as I was wondering if the mere sight of someone could produce such energized feelings of joy, just as I was wondering if I had really seen him and whether the whole thing was not part of some dream, Jayalakshmi appeared and said, "Wasn't it nice of Baba to give you such a look?" It certainly was.

The days fell into a rhythmic pattern of meditation, darshan and bhajans. At 4:45 A.M. devotees gather in the prayer hall, called the Mandir, to chant OM 21 times. After the Omkar pundits and musicians chant the Suprabhatam, a prayer for the awakening of the Lord within each individual. This is followed by the singing of devotional songs called bhajans. Women walk in one direction, men in another, their songs consecrating the morning air as the sun rises above the surrounding hills.

Adjustment to the routine came easily due to several kind and generous women. I had arrived with a letter of introduction from Indra Devi to Kanwarani Balbir Kaur, known to her pupils among the schoolboys at the ashram school as Mataji, revered mother. Daily she offered me lunch, answered my questions, and gave me a cool spot under her ceiling fan for my afternoon nap.

The morning of my fourth day I was called to the interview room with several women devotees from New Delhi and a dozen young college girls from the Sathya Sai Baba College for Woman at Anantapur, about 2 hours away by car. Up to now Baba had looked in my direction, sometimes smiling, once asking how I was, but this was my first opportunity to be in his presence for any length of time.

Baba spoke mostly to the women from Delhi about their health and family problems. I sat there understanding some but not much of the conversation, happy to just be able to see him so closely and hear the tender cadence of a voice expressing such love. I had seen the majestic, paternal, almost regal attitude exuded by Baba during public darshan as he walked among the crowds with a gliding motion that seemed to carry him effortlessly over the ground. Now I was witnessing his loving and maternal nature as he filled every heart in the room with intangible, inexpressible fullness.

I sat transfixed, unaware that I was fingering the pendant Dick had brought back for me when Baba turned from the ladies, looked at me and asked if I would like HIM to give me a pendant. He waited calmly as I took in the question, my eyes glued to his face while I silently nodded, yes. Then his hand stretched out, moved in a circular pattern with palm open in clear view of everyone in the room. His fingers closed for an instant and when he opened them there was a silver medallion slightly larger than a quarter, complete with a ring on which to hang it from a chain. He put it into my hands and I saw first his image raised on the silver with the words, "Why fear when I am here," spelled out in English. He then told me to turn it over where I saw an image of Sai Baba of Shirdi and the inscription, also in English, "If you look to me I look to you."

After pronouncing the inscriptions for us all, Baba stood, indicating the interview was concluding. As he did so, he again waved his hand, producing a quantity of vibuthi which he gave to each of us as we reluctantly filed out of the room.

The interview over, I walked into the prayer hall where bhajans were being sung, and for the next hour sat holding my new silver medallion, marveling at wonders beyond my comprehension. I couldn't help but reflect on what I had just seen and contrast it with the scepticism I had heard people express when hearing about Baba's miracles, or as he calls them, leelas, meaning divine play, especially those who insist the objects are up his sleeve or in his hair. But I had found they stopped insisting once they realized the phenomenon began when Baba was a tiny child and not only did he materialize and give away objects of value unknown in the remote village which like so many others was frequently impoverished by capricious weather conditions, his entire early years were spent helping others. And how, in spite of warnings from his father and an unbelievably painful attempt by his well meaning family to exorcise the "demons" by cutting open his scalp with knives and pouring lye into the wounds when he was fourteen, the materializations continued.

In that moment it was not the materialization of the object itself that mattered but the fact that I now possessed a tangible link which had passed from his hand to mine symbolizing our relationship. The medal said, "If you look to me I look to you," a promise of constancy. And, "Why fear when I am here," not "I" in the limited personal sense but "I" in totality, the principle behind all manifestations, even the form of Baba himself. It was a challenge to recognize the all-pervasive nature of God and live free of the most limiting and confining aspect of human nature, fear. Now if only I could keep these words in my head and heart as well as on a chain around my neck.

Toward the end of my first week people began arriving for the festival called Maha-Sivarathri, one of the major holy days of the year. It is held all over India on the day of the new moon between February and March. The dark of the moon is important because the moon is recognized as the presiding deity of the mind—and when it is full the mind is rampant, hence the Western use of the word lunatic. When the reflected light from the moon is reduced to a slender arc the mind is calm and worldly tendencies can be more easily overcome through spiritual practices. Each year this day and night are set aside for meditation, fasting and singing the name of God.

At Prasanthi Nilayam, in Sai Baba's presence, Sivarathri takes on added meaning. For many years a unique ceremony has taken place called the Lingodbhava, at which time Baba brings forth the one or more lingams materialized inside his body. These lingams have appeared as elliptically-shaped stones of varying clarity and color, sometimes as much as 3 or 4 inches in length. They symbolize the manifestation of the unmanifest, that moment when the infinite becomes finite in the form recognized as the seed or egg out of which new life, in this case new spiritual life, is born.

During an afternoon visit with Balbir she told me of the Sivarathri festival two years earlier when Baba gave the lingam to her stepdaughter, Her Highness, Maharani Prithivi Bir Kaur of Jind, whom she was expecting to arrive at any time. Several things struck me about Prithivi when we met, her name in Sanskrit meaning earth or world, primarily her great vitality expressed through an impish wit, a pair of dark flashing eyes and a beautiful smile. It seems strange even now to think that someone like myself from a working class family in Southern California could have much in common with someone raised as royalty in an exotic Eastern land, but soon we were talking and laughing, sharing past joys and sorrows like a pair of reunited college roommates.

The first function of the festival day was the ceremonial

flag-raising from the top of the mandir, followed by the Vibuthi Abhishekam in the rectangular pavilion with open sides called the auditorium. I had responded to a call for volunteers to help with the festival crowds, and after two days of chopping vegetables in the canteen and sweeping the grounds with a short handled broom, I was now positioned in the auditorium on the ladies' side of the center aisle, about ten rows from the front with instructions to see the crowds did not push forward.

The auditorium filled up for the morning ceremony and still more people came. I saw Prithivi on the outside and signaled for her to join me. She managed to pass through the crowd and I inched over to give her the seat on the aisle. The bhajan leaders began to sing. All eyes held to the spot where Baba was to enter. It was then my emotional catchbasin began to overflow. The part of my mind which was viewing the symbolism and pageantry, and trying to keep a rational perspective, came face-to-face with something much more powerful. I suddenly felt as well as saw the overwhelming outpouring of silent spiritual energy generated between Baba and the immense crowd.

He appeared in the distance, walking slowly to the center aisle, then back to the far end of the pavilion, all the while turning from side to side, hands raised in blessing. Tears began to flow and try as I might they would not be stopped. The best I could manage was to pull the end of my sari up over my head and wipe my eyes with the end of it.

Baba approached, his glance sweeping the crowds. Next to me, Prithivi was hoping for some special recognition and I thought I would at least be there to see it. I gave my eyes one last swipe with the sari and looked up as he stepped past us, his glance taking in the vast numbers. Then, before I knew what happened, his head turned and, for an instant his eyes riveted mine with a look of undiluted power. As I felt the charge my emotion was transmuted into calm. Prithivi, turning to me with a look of mock indignation, laughingly whispered, "You gave me your seat and you got my look."

But there was no time to wonder or comment. Baba had reached the center of the stage and was standing next to a silver statue of Sai Baba of Shirdi. One of the pundits was holding a basin of water and Baba had rolled up both of his sleeves to the elbow and begun ceremonially bathing the statue before wiping it dry.

Prithivi had prepared me for the possibility Baba might manifest some talisman to place on the statue as he had done before. She had come prepared with a small pair of binoculars and was watching his every move. At what seemed to be a lull she handed them to me for a quick look. As I raised them to my eyes Baba's hand began to move and as the statue came into focus I clearly saw manifest in the space between the thumb and forefinger of his empty right hand a small gold setting of eight deep red stones, surrounding a ninth stone in the center. As soon as it appeared Baba pressed it against the forehead of the statue, where it remained. I immediately returned the binoculars.

Now Mr. Kasturi appeared holding an urn about 18 inches tall. This was to be the Vibuthi Abhishekam, the ceremonial bathing of the statue with ash to symbolize the ultimate state of all physical matter.

The empty urn was upturned over the statue. Nothing happened. Then Baba inserted his right hand into it and vibuthi began to flow and flow and flow. The ash first covered the statue, then the base it rested on, and finally was even streaming into the audience. The lucky ones in front hurriedly collecting it while the rest of us inhaled its fragrance. When, after several more minutes, the soft, sweet-smelling ash seemed to be everywhere and Baba's arms and robe were white with it, he raised his right hand to the audience, smiled and disappeared through the back curtain. When the audience realized he had gone there was a wave-like motion rising and pressing toward the stage, with all of us carried in its wake.

Throughout the ashram a sense of gathering prevailed, like the mainspring of some enormous timepiece, the universe itself perhaps. Busses had arrived in the night and whole villages had walked for miles. Sivarathri is also a day for silence and fasting so instead of the midday meal we rested and waited for the birth of the lingam.

The evening function was to take place outdoors before a raised octagonal platform called the Shanti Vedica, beautifully painted with scenes from the Bhagavad Gita. It began with speeches by devotees. Then Baba spoke about the unifying aspect of God at the core of each atom in the universe. He spoke also of the elimination of the ego. He said:

> The elimination of the identification with the body and its needs, satisfiable through the senses, is the main point of life. For you get the joy when these needs are fulfilled; grief when they are not, anger when something comes in the way, pride when you win over that opposition. To eliminate the ego, strengthen the belief that all objects belong to God, and that you are holding them on trust. This would prevent pride, it is also the truth. Then, when you lose a thing you would not grieve. God gave, God took away. Of course you hear almost all talking in this strain and advising this reaction. But very few follow that advice themselves. This is the sin of all sins: saying one thing and acting quite the opposite, denying in practice what you assert as precept.

After the speech was concluded Baba began to sing. A few minutes later he coughed, then sat down. The bhajan leaders took up the chant. He sipped water from a cup, occasionally wiping his brow. The spasms Baba was feeling were now visible as his throat constricted again and again. Then, as he held a white handkerchief in his outstretched hands we all saw a stream of light emerge from his mouth. He

179

caught it and held it up. It was the lingam. Opalescent, smooth, lit from within, alive with the essence as well as the symbolism of divinity.

After the birth of the lingam devotees maintained an all-night vigil of bhajan singing. At dawn Baba appeared for darshan and later in the morning he returned to distribute the ash from the Vibuthi Abhishekam which had been wrapped in small folded squares of paper by volunteers. Hour after hour he walked through the curving rows of devotees seated in front of the prayer hall and everywhere the ground was flat. I watched on and off during those hours. The immense numbers of people no longer impressed me, what moved me was Baba, giving, hand to hand, to the thousands who sat in silence. The sleeves of his robe were rolled up to his elbows, perspiration was causing the fabric to cling to his chest and back, as he moved relentlessly through the crowd. I had heard him say, "I am your servant." Now I saw this was true.

With the festival over, the crowds gradually dispersed. When Baba left for a brief visit to the college at Anantapur, I returned to Bangalore where I met a small group of western devotees, among them Howard and Iris Murphet who were researching the book Howard would later write called "Sai Baba—Man of Miracles."

Baba returned to Brindavan, his residence just outside Bangalore and the Murphets received word that our small group should come out each morning. Those hours have run together in my memory, but certain moments are clear. Much of the conversation was between Baba and Mr. and Mrs. Murphet, while the rest of us looked on. He spoke of meditation, the importance of discipline, and how we confuse love and lust. He spoke about how brief moments of anger consume the life force energy of many months in just a few minutes. He compared the human body to Murali, the Sanskrit name for Lord Krishna's flute, and explained the importance of making our minds and bodies pure, symbolically hollow like the flute, so that the Lord can then use them to make beautiful music.

Day after day I sat listening to Baba answer my unspoken questions, drinking in his nearness. But now my time was almost up, the visit nearly over. I was scheduled to fly to Bombay Friday afternoon and by Thursday night I admitted to myself I had one question for which his words were necessary, no inner prompting or feeling would suffice.

The next morning I brought along a roll of three large photographs I was hoping to have signed and when I held them up as Baba entered the room, he smiled and said, "You are not leaving yet." So I sat quietly while others asked questions. After about 30 minutes he stood, waved his right hand and began to distribute something to each person from his hand. Inexplicable though it seems, he had manifested pieces of sweet pastry which crumbled into our hands still warm. The taste was delicate, the texture creamy, the astonishment complete.

Next he looked at me and said in a statement that was also a question, "You lead bhajans." I blurted out that we sang along with the tapes and the record. He then asked us to sing for him. A look of desperation went around the room as he smiled patiently. Iris Murphet and I looked at one another and began one of the more simple bhajans. The others soon joined in and Baba watched intently as we tried to sing the right melody and pronounce the words correctly.

Again he stood and waved his hand, but this time he held up the object he had materialized to those on the other side of the room and I couldn't see what it was until, that is, he turned toward me and put it into my hand. It was a colored enamel pendant with his image set in a coppery bronze metal. Before I could react he motioned for me to come with him into the next room. He also asked Nanda, a young Indian woman, to act as translator.

Nanda and I followed him to the far side of the small room where he immediately began to speak. After giving me a detailed message for a devotee in California, he paused and indicated I could now ask my question. Rather than speak, and stalling for time, I held up the photographs. He picked up a pen and signed each one with an inscription, his name and the date, 20th March, 1970. As he finished the third one he looked at me and said in English, as if to remind me that the signing of the photos was just a gesture, "But I am in your heart." The look in his eyes as he spoke reached deep inside me and with a searing fire seemed to burn off the emotional scar tissue left by the pain, fear and hurt of an endless number of past lifetimes.

Again he asked for my question. I had thought long and hard about it and so, taking a deep breath, I began. "Baba," I asked, "you know Dick Bock?" He said he did.

I took another breath and plunged ahead. "Baba, if, sometime in the future, we should decide to get married, would we have your blessing?"

His reply came instantly. "Yes," he said, "but quickly, quickly."

I couldn't believe what I was hearing. The look tele-graphed my disbelief and I blurted out my gut feeling, "Baba, I can't say that to a man."

He made a fist with his right hand, gesturing as if pounding a gavel. "It's truth," he said.

I looked at Nanda, somehow thinking the translation of the words would be different, forgetting in the momentary dismay that he had spoken to me in English.

Now my head was really spinning. "When is quickly?" I asked.

"Before July!"

In the next moment he looked through my eyes into my heart and said, "I am always with you. Santosh, very happy," and walked out to join the others. I followed, carrying the pictures, and sat down. Baba spoke a few more words, manifested vibuthi from his hand for me as a final good-bye and left the room.

Everyone was anxious to see the pendant and to help me find something to carry the ash in my hand. Nanda showed me how to wrap it up and I put the remainder on the center of my forehead. As I was walking out the driveway with the Murphets, Mr. Ramabrahma, the jolly man who has the responsibility for running the household at Brindavan, came hurrying out with prasad, it was blessed fruit from Baba.

The Murphets dropped me at the airport where I discovered a strike by the local airline would keep me in Bangalore an extra night and force me to change all on-going flight reservations. The next day in Bombay Kamala listened to my account of the trip. Dear Kamala could see my confusion and understood how difficult it would be for me to convey Baba's words to Dick, what a blow to the pride of any woman who had grown up with the Western idea of marriage and the belief that it was somehow shameful if the man were not the one to propose.

We had 12 hours to spend before my flight, so after lunch she suggested we visit the temple of Ganesha we had passed on my first visit. I was willing to do anything that might take my mind off my dilemma. We arrived at the temple and bought fresh coconuts at the gate. Inside there were few people and in the dim light I watched so I would know what to do. The Pujari, the man who performed the puja ceremony, accepted the coconuts, cracked them with a knife and poured the pure coconut water over the little elephant-headed idol of Ganesha. If Ganesha could help me overcome the obstacle of pride which now loomed so large in front of me and filled my mind with confusion and agitation, I was ready.

I handed my coconut to the pujari, stepped back and closed my eyes. The inner darkness suddenly was filled with the image of a blackboard covered with equations and formulas which, as I watched, was wiped clean with the wide sweeping motion of an eraser. Stroke by stroke the mathematical problems were wiped away, the scribblings of trying to figure them out were gone and I was left with a clean slate, literally. With the half-figured equations went the chaotic emotions and as I stood there I could once again take a deep breath. It seemed later as though in that moment something had been resolved on a deep subconscious level, even though my mind did not understand the process at the time.

I filled my lungs with the temple smells, wondering what had just happened. Then I looked at Kamala who just smiled and led me out into the sunlight.

The flight from Bombay to Los Angeles seemed unending, especially since I had no way of knowing if the message about my new arrival time had been received. Somewhere over the mid-west I was again pondering Baba's message. Could I bring myself to tell Dick? If I could it would have to be soon because to bring it up later would seem contrived.

The plane landed and Indra Devi appeared. She explained Dick had asked her to meet me because he was flying in from a recording date in Las Vegas and would be arriving in 20 minutes. While we waited for my luggage I briefly explained what Baba had said. Just then Dick appeared and our reunion was complete. I showed him my silver medallion and the enamel pendant and we made plans to get proper chains for each of them.

We said good-bye to Indra Devi and started toward Hollywood. The further we drove the louder I could hear Baba's voice saying, "It's truth!"

So, with a deep breath I began softly, "There was one question I asked in my interview with Baba."

"Oh," Dick replied, unsuspectingly.

"I asked if sometime in the future we should decide to get married . . ."

Before I could continue Dick interrupted, "You know, I've been thinking about that." Then he smiled and said questioningly, "Would you consider yourself engaged?"

The following Sunday was Easter and for me Jesus had never been more alive. The resurrection was a fact, the Jesus

The two pendants materialized by Bhagavan Sri
Sathya Sai Baba for the author in 1970.

Bhagavan Sri Sathya Sai Baba, and Janet and Richard
Bock.

Bhagavan Sri Sathya Sai Baba

of my childhood innocence existed once again, not as Sathya Sai Baba, but as an emanation from the same source. I now knew everyone and every thing was a part of God, even me. I not only had the philosophical framework with which to accept it intellectually, but I had been graced with an experience calling that recognition forth from deep within. I was beginning to experience a realm beyond the sectarian limitations I had always known, a realm where unity was real and separation of faiths, of peoples, was the illusion.

I have a favorite passage in a discourse by Baba in which he explains his role in this unity.

"I have come to light the lamp of love in your hearts, to see that it shines day by day with added lustre. I have not come to speak on behalf of any teaching, like the Hindu teaching. I have not come on any mission of publicity for any sect or creed or cause; nor have I come to collect the followers for any doctrine. I have no plan to attract disciples or devotees into my fold or any fold. I have come to tell you of this universal unitary faith, this Atmic principle, this path of love, this duty of love, this obligation to love.

"All religions teach one basic discipline; the removal from the mind of the blemish of egoism of running after little joys. Every religion teaches man to fill his being with the glory of God and evict the pettiness of conceit. It trains him in the methods of detachment and discrimination so that he may aim high and attain liberation.

"Believe that all hearts are motivated by the One and Only God; that all faiths glorify the One Only God, that all names in all languages and all forms man can conceive denote the One and Only God; His adoration is best done by means of love. Cultivate that attitude of Oneness between men of all creeds, all countries and all continents. That is the message of love I bring. That is the message I wish you to take to heart."[1]

On another occasion Sai Baba spoke at length about Jesus.

"The followers of each religion call upon the One God, who is Omnipresent and who listens to their prayers from whichever clime or clothed in whatever language; but, it is the same God who confers upon all mankind health, prosperity, peace and happiness. Each religion has no separate God showering Grace upon those who profess to abide by that faith alone!

"It is the destiny of man to journey from 'humanness' to divinity, as he has already journeyed from 'animal-ness.' In this pilgrimage he is bound to encounter various obstacles and trials. In order to smoothen his path and help him overcome these troubles, sages, seers, realised souls, divine personalities and Incarnations of God appear among men and illumine the path. They move among the afflicted, the seekers who have lost their way or strayed into the desert, and lead them into confidence and courage. Certain personalities are born and live out their days for this very purpose. They can be called Karana-janmas for they assume the janma or birth for a karana or cause or purpose. Such guides, exemplars, and leaders appear among all peoples and in all lands. They inspire faith in higher ideals, and teach, as if their voice is the voice of God, counseling from the heart.

"Of course, there are many aspirants who by their devotion, dedication and disciplined lives attain the Vision of the Omnipresent, Omnipotent and Omniscient ONE. They are content with the bliss they have won for themselves. Others there are who long to share their bliss with those beyond the pale; they guide and lead and are blessed thereby. They teach that multiplicity is a delusion that Unity is the Reality. They instruct others that each one is really three in one; the one he believes he is, the one others believe he is, and the one he really is.

"Jesus was a karana-janma, a Master born with a purpose, the mission of restoring Love, Charity and Compassion in the heart of man. He had no attachment to the self; he never paid heed to sorrow or pain, joy or gain; he had a heart that responded to the call of anguish, the cry for peace and brother-hood. He went about the land, preaching the lesson of Love, and poured out his life as a libation in the sacrifice to humanity.

"Like most seekers, he searched for the Divine in the objective world in nature, but he soon realized that nature is a kaleidoscopic picture, created by one's own imagination, and sought God within himself. Here, his stay in the Himalayan monasteries, in Kashmir and other centres of eastern asceticism and philosophical inquiry brought him greater success. From the attitude of being a Messenger of God, he declared that he was the Son of God, after returning from the East. For the old attitude meant duality, a master-servant relationship. One could not then move beyond the orders of the Master. One had to carry out the duties laid down in the scriptures of the faith. This he found too irksome and he felt he was the image, while God was the original.

"The bond of relationship increased, the I was no more in some distant light or entity; the light became a part of the I. With body-consciousness predominant, you feel you are a servant or messenger. With heart-consciousness in the ascendant, you feel near-

ness and dear-ness and so the son-father bond seems
natural at this stage. Later as the soul-consciousness
became stabilized, Jesus could declare, 'I and my
Father are One,' just as one states, I was in the Light,
then, the Light was in me, and now I am aware that
I am the Light.

"Jesus could assert that his life was his message
for he lived among men as he advised them to. Everyone has to start his spiritual pilgrimage, proclaiming
that he is a servant of God or a messenger of God and
trying to live up to that high and responsible status.
This is the stage of Duality. Then he progresses to
discover the Divine within himself, and realises that
God is his precious heritage, which he must claim and
utilise. That is the stage when one feels he is a son of
God, of the same nature as God. Finally, he merges in
God-consciousness. This is the essence of all religious
disciplines and teachings.

"Jesus was the name he was known by; he was
honoured by the populace as Christ, for they found
in his thoughts, deeds and words no trace of ego. He
had no envy or hatred; he was full of love and
charity, humility and sympathy. The name Jesus
itself is not the original one. He was named Isa, which
with the letters reversed is Sai. Isa or Sai both mean
'Isvara,' God, the Eternal Absolute, the Sath-Chith-
Ananda (existence, knowledge, bliss). In the Tibetan
manuscript at the monastery where Isa spent some
years the name is written as Issa. The name Isa means
the Lord of all Living Beings.

"When Jesus proclaimed that he was the Messenger of God, he wanted to emphasise that every one is
a messenger of God and has to speak, act and think as
one. This is the true Karma Kanda of the Vedas, the
spiritual discipline of work, of repetition of the name
of the Lord, of meditation, of service. When progress

is furthered, Jesus asserted, each one can recognise all as Sons of God, Children of God, brothers and sisters of oneself and so, deserving of worship. Finally, knowledge ripens into wisdom and the goal is reached when each one realises 'I and my Father are One.'

"The Birthday of Jesus must be celebrated by all mankind for such Masters belong to the whole human race. They should not be confined to a single country or community. Jesus found that scholars and ritualists had befogged the true religion. He engaged himself in teaching both spirituality and morality, for education is the very Light of Life. Jesus found that people were running after glass beads and, imagining them to be diamonds, were attaching great value for them. He went round the holy shrines and discovered that they had become bazaars where Grace was being bargained for and commercialised. He condemned the priesthood which tolerated and encouraged these practices. So, he drew upon himself the anger of the heads of the temples and monasteries. They tempted one of the disciples of Jesus with 30 pieces of silver to betray him into their hands.

"The Roman rulers were told that Jesus was attempting to assert himself as King and so could be punished for treason. Their insistence made the Governor order his crucifixion. When the nails were being driven into him to fix him on the Cross, Jesus heard the Voice of the Father saying, 'All life is one, my dear son! Be alike to every one,' and he pleaded that those who were crucifying him may be pardoned for they knew not what they did. Jesus sacrificed himself for the sake of mankind.

"Carols and candles, readings from the Bible and acting out the incidents that surrounded his birth are not enough to celebrate the birth of Jesus. Jesus said that the bread taken in the last supper was his flesh, and the wine his blood. He meant that all beings alive with flesh and blood are to be treated as he himself and that no distinction should be made as friend or foe, we and they. Every body is his body, sustained by the bread; every drop of blood flowing in the veins of every living being is his, animated by the activity that the wine imparted to it. That is to say, every man and woman is Divine and has to be revered as such.

"You work as a messenger or servant; later, you worship, as a son does his father, and finally, you achieve the wisdom that you and He are One. That is the spiritual journey, and Jesus has shown the way in clear terms. He announced very early in life that he had come to illumine the spiritual path. He had the Light within him.

"To elevate man, to raise the level of his consciousness, God has to incarnate as Man. He has to speak to them in their own style and languages, he has to teach them the methods that they can adopt and practise. Birds and beasts need no Divine Incarnation as birds or beasts to guide them for they have no inclination to stray away from their path. Man alone forgets or ignores the goal of life."[2]

Sathya Sai Baba's ashram, Prasanthi Nilayam, as it appeared in 1970.

192

Chapter XVIII

AGAIN AND AGAIN AND AGAIN

That mankind has forgotten and ignored the goal of life becomes clear when one studies the major religions and sees that the same message has been repeated again and again throughout the ages. It becomes apparent that religion is the cultural manifestation of a spiritual experience so basic that every society on earth has created a form for its expression. Because of the differences in culture created by environment and history, it is natural for each society to have developed or modified its own expression of what is, in essence, the same inner experience.

The Vedas of India, including the Upanishads, are the oldest writings known on earth. The Mahabharata and the Bhagavad Gita relate the life and teachings of Lord Krishna who lived centuries before the stories were written down. Moses lived approximately 1600 B.C., Zoroaster lived more than 600 years before Christ. Confucius was born in 600 B.C. and Gautama Buddha in 563 B.C. Jesus lived from 1 to 33 A.D. and Mohammed was born in 570 A.D.

We can choose to perceive them as separate scattered voices calling out through time, or we can recognize the sound of the Lord speaking through His incarnations.

CREATION

In the beginning the Lord of the Universe alone existed. With Him the word was the second, and the world is verily the Supreme Brahman (God).[1]

—From the Brahmanas of the Vedas

In the beginning was the Word, and the Word was with God, and the Word was God; the same was in the beginning with God.[2]

—The Bible, John 1:1

THE GOLDEN RULE

Do not to others what ye do not wish
Done to yourself; and wish for others too
What ye desire and long for, for yourself.
This is the whole of righteousness, heed it well.[3]

—The Mahabharata

That which is good for all and any one,
For whomsoever—that is good for me. . . .
What I hold good for self, I should for all.
Only Law Universal is true law.[4]

—Zoroaster

When abroad, behave to everyone as if interviewing an honored guest; in directing the people, act as if you were assisting at a great sacrifice; DO NOT DO TO OTHERS AS YOU WOULD NOT LIKE DONE TO YOURSELF: so there will be no murmuring against you in the country, and none in the family; your public life will arouse no ill-will nor your private life any resentment.[5]

—Confucius

What is hateful to thee, do not unto thy fellowman; this is the whole Law. The rest is but commentary.[6]
—Hillel the Elder, a sage of Judaism

Do unto others as you would have others do unto you.[7]
—The Bible

WORSHIP

Whatever thou doest, whatever thou eatest, whatever thou offerest in sacrifice, whatever thou givest away, whatever austerity thou practicest, do that as an offering unto me.[8]
—Lord Krishna, Bhagavad Gita IX:27

Whatever your task, work heartily, as serving the Lord and not men, knowing that from the Lord you will receive the inheritance as your reward; you are serving the Lord Christ.[9]
—Colossians 3:23

GRACE

I am the origin of everything, everything arises out of Me; by knowing this men offer everything to Me and worship Me with loving devotion.[10]
—Lord Krishna, Bhagavad Gita X:8

I am the bread of life: he that cometh to me shall never hunger, and he that believeth on me shall never thirst.[11]
—Jesus Christ, John 6:35

195

Persons who are so devoted to Me that their whole heart and mind go unto Me without thinking of anything else, they who worship Me in all beings and meditate on Me; out of grace I guard what they have and I secure what they have not; their welfare is assured through Me.[12]

—Lord Krishna, Bhagavad Gita XI:22

KINGDOM OF GOD, KINGDOM OF HEAVEN

That which the organ of speech cannot apprehend, but which apprehends the organ of speech, that is Brahman, the Supreme Reality, shining in the heart.

That which the mind cannot apprehend but which apprehends the mind;
That which the eyes cannot see, but which perceives the eyes, because of which the eyes see; that which the ears cannot hear, but which perceives the ears, because of which the ears hear;
That which the nose cannot smell, but because of which the nose has the power of smelling—know that to be the Supreme Reality, ever dwelling within you.[13]

—Kena Upanishad 1:5-9

The Kingdom of God cometh not with observation; neither shall they say, Lo here or, lo there! for behold, the Kingdom of God is within you.[14]

—Jesus Christ, Luke 17:20, 21

The kingdom of heaven is like unto leaven, which a woman took and hid in three measures of meal, till the whole was leavened.[15]

—Jesus Christ, Matt. 13:33

NON-RESISTANCE

Even though scolded by the wicked or insulted, ridiculed, calumniated, beaten, bound, robbed of his living or spat upon or otherwise abominably treated by the ignorant—being thus variously shaken and placed in dire extremities, the man who desires his well-being should deliver himself by his own effort through patience and non-resistance.[16]

—Lord Krishna, Bhagavantam XI:22, 57, 58

Let a man overcome anger by love, let him overcome evil by good; let him overcome the greedy by generosity, and a liar by the truth. For hatred does not cease by hatred at any time; hatred ceases by love, this is an old rule.[17]

—Gautama Buddha, Dhammapada, vs. 5

Resist not evil.

Love your enemies.

Bless them that persecute you.[18]

—Jesus Christ

PURITY OF HEART

If we liberate our hearts from petty selfishness, wish no ill to others, and become clear as a crystal reflecting the light of truth, what a radiant picture will appear in us mirroring things as they are, without the admixture of burning desires, without the distortion of erroneous illusion, without the agitation of sinful unrest.[19]

—Gautama Buddha

That happiness which belongs to a mind which by deep meditation has been washed clean from all impurity and has entered within the higher Self, cannot be described here by words, it can be felt by the inward power only.[20]

—Brahmana Upanishad

Blessed are the pure in heart for they shall see God.[21]

—Jesus Christ

LOVE OF MAN

When a person abstains from doing wrong to any creature, in thought, word, or deed, he is said to attain the state of oneness with God.[22]

—Mahabharata, p. 127

He who hates no creature and is friendly and compassionate to all, who is free from attachment and egotism, equal-minded in pleasure and pain, and forgiving; who is ever content and meditative, self-subjugated and possessed with firm conviction, with mind and intellect dedicated to Me, he who is thus devoted to Me is dear to Me.[23]

—Teachings of Lord Krishna

You must so adjust your heart that you long for the welfare of all beings, including the happiness of your enemies. If a man foolishly does me wrong, I will return to him the protection of my ungrudging love; the more evil comes from him, the more good shall go from me. . . Let us live happily then, not hating those who hate us. Among men who hate us let us dwell free from hatred. . . With pure thoughts and fulness of love, I will do towards others what I would do for myself.[24]

—Lord Buddha

To the good I would be good. To the not-good I would also be good in order to make them good. Recompense injury with kindness. . . Of all noble qualities, loving compassion is the noblest.[25]

—Laotze

The good man loves all men. He loves to speak of the good of others. All within the four seas are his brothers. Love of man is the chief of all the virtues. . . The mean man sows, that himself or his friends may reap; but the love of the perfect man is universal.[26]

—Confucius

Love your enemies, bless them that curse you, do good to them that hate you, and pray for them that despitefully use you, and persecute you; that ye may be the children of your Father which is in Heaven . . . Do unto others what ye would have others do unto you.[27]

—Jesus the Christ

DIVINE INCARNATIONS

Many lives have I passed through, as also yourself. Many times have I been born, but I know all this. You do not know because you are an ordinary mortal under the spell of ignorance. I am a divine person. I know how many times I have been born.

Though I am birthless, of changeless nature and Lord of beings, I am born in human form through my own inscrutable power.

Whenever righteousness declines and unrighteousness prevails, I body myself forth, assume human form, and live as a human being.

199

In order to protect the righteous and also to punish the wicked, I incarnate Myself on this earth from time to time.[28]

—Lord Krishna, Bhagavad Gita IV:5, 6, 7, 8

... for I proceeded forth and came from God; neither came I of myself but he sent me.[29]

—Jesus Christ, John 8:42

ANGER

He who restrains his rage from bolting with him,
He is true warrior and true charioteer,
Not he that slays in battle many foes.[30]

—The Mahabharata

Repay not blow by blow, nor curse by curse,
Nor by base trick the meanest craftiness;
But shower blessings in return for blows
And curses and mean craftiness, all.[31]

—Bhagavad Gita

Recompense injury with kindness.[32]

—Lao-tse

Recompense injury with justice, and return good for good.[33]

—Confucius

Love your enemies, bless them that curse you, do good to them that hate you, and pray for them which despitefully use you and persecute you.[34]

—Jesus Christ

SELF-CONTROL

With kindness conquer rage; with goodness malice;
With generosity defeat all meanness;
With the straight truth defeat lies and deceit.[35]

—Mahabharata

Conquer hatred with love.[36]

—Gautama Buddha

Conquer your wrath by sweet forgivingness;
And by humility check vanity;
By truth straightforward stay all crooked fraud;
And by contentment peaceful, vanquish greed.[37]

—Jain Sacred Writings

If thine enemy be hungry, give him bread; if he be
thirsty, give him water; so shalt thou heap coals of
fire upon his head; and so the Lord shall award thee;
for thy enemy will feel ashamed of his hostile feeling,
and his head, his face, will "burn" with shame, and he
will give up enmity and become thy friend, and that
will be thy great reward.[38]

—Proverbs

Resist not evil; if any smite thee on the right cheek,
turn the left to him as well. . . Bless them that curse
you; love your enemies and pray for those who
persecute you.[39]

—Jesus Christ

PRAYER

Supreme Lord of Warmth and Light
of life and consciousness, that knowest all!
Guide us by the Right Path to happiness!

And give us strength and will to war against
The sins that rage in us and lead us astray!
We bow in reverence and prayer to thee![40]

— Vedas

Blessed Lord! O High Deliverer!
Source of all Wisdom, Fountain of all Light!
I take my refuge in Thy name and Thee!
I take my refuge in Thy Law of Good!
I take my refuge in Thy Order! Aum!
The gem-like drop of dew—my little soul—
May it pass into the Lotus-bloom that floats
Upon the Sea of Thy Infinity![41]

— Buddhist Prayer

Hear, O Israel! the Lord is our God, the Lord is One.
May it be Thy will, O Lord our God, and God of our
fathers, to cause us to walk in Thy law and cleave to
Thy commandments; and lead us not into sin,
transgression, temptation, and contempt. Remove
from us every evil inclination and cause us to adhere
to the good. Oh, grant us grace, favour and mercy in
Thy sight, and in the sight of all that beholds us, and
bestow gracious favors on us. Blessed art Thou,
O Lord, who bestowest gracious favours on Thy
People Israel.[42]

— Jewish Prayer

Our Father which art in heaven
Hallowed be Thy name. Thy kingdom come,
Thy will be done on earth as it is in heaven.
Give us this day our daily bread,
and Forgive us our debts, as we forgive our debtors.
And lead us not into temptation; but deliver us from evil.
For Thine is the kingdom, and the power, and the glory,
Forever. Amen![43]

— Christian Prayer

Praise be unto the Lord of all the worlds!
O Lord of Mercy and Beneficence!
Master Supreme of the great Judgment day!
Thee do we serve and Thee beseech for help;
Show us the Path on which Thy blessings rest,
The Straight Path; not of those who go astray,
On whom descends thy wrath and punishment.[44]

—Moslem Prayer

UNIVERSALITY

Cows are of many colours, but milk is of one color,
white;
So the proclaimers who proclaim the Truth
Use many varying forms to put it in,
But yet the Truth enclosed in all is One.[45]

—Upanishads

To but One Goal are marching everywhere,
All human beings, though they may seem to walk
On paths divergent; and that Goal is I,
The Universal Self, Self-Consciousness.[46]

—Krishna, Bhagavad Gita

And we worship the former religions of the world
devoted to righteousness.[47]

—Zoroaster

I only hand on; I cannot create new things.[48]

—Confucius

Is there anything whereof it may be said, see, this is
new? It hath been already of old time, which was
before us. . . There is no new thing under the sun.[49]

—Ecclesiastes

I come not to destroy the law or the prophets but to fulfill them.[50]

—Jesus Christ

This that I am now uttering unto you,
The Holy Quran—it is to be found
Within the ancient Seers' writings too;
For Teachers have been sent to every race.
Of human beings no community
Is left without a warner and a guide.
And aught of difference we do not make—
For disagreement there is none 'twixt them—
Between these Prophets. All that have been sent
Have been so sent but One Truth to proclaim—
"I verily the I All-One, am God,
There is no other God than I, (the Self,
The Universal all-pervading Self),
And I alone should be adored by all."[51]

—Koran

* * * * * * * *

The Jesus Mystery is our mystery, too. For each of us is living with the chance to fill and fulfill a lifetime we innately know is not some fluke of nature, but God given. If we cannot leave home to wander foreign lands ourselves, we can follow the path of Saint Issa, and our own instincts.

From the Jains Issa observed and came to know the sanctity of all life. Sacrifice was no longer the slaughter of innocents. Human thoughts, words and actions were to be made sacred by purifying and offering them to God. The remnants of man's animal past, hatred, jealousy, lust, greed, anger and fear, conditions once important in a world where fight or flight determined survival, were no longer appropriate in human beings capable of higher thought. In the solitude of the Jain caves came the realization that these vestigial traits have to be recognized, made sacred through inner purification and finally sacrificed in order to merge with and experience the non-violent nature of ultimate reality.

During the years in India Issa encountered Karma and saw how the law of cause and effect returned all thoughts, words and actions to their source in precise measure.

Within the temple of the Lord of the Universe he recognized that all are equal in the eyes of God, in spite of priestly teachings of class, sex, creed or caste, and he preached this truth to the oppressed without concern for his own safety.

He saw that as the wheel of life turns the integrity of the soul remains whether in life or death. He saw that events of one life determine those of the next, that heredity and environment are secondary to past actions in determining our situation today. He came to know that lasting satisfaction can never come from objects of the impermanent material world, and that death is nothing to fear.

He studied the science of yoga for the purpose of merging his consciousness with that of the creator. For the rest of his life he used the miraculous abilities which came as a result of this process with love and compassion to help those in need. There is no evidence he ever used them for himself. Even when death was imminent he allowed it to come, then not only triumphed over it, but left his burial shroud to project his mystery down through the ages.

Issa learned that God is not the sole province of any one group or religion, but can be found by experiencing the truth at the core of each faith.

Finally, Issa found that the Lord is not standing apart from us handing out punishment and retribution, but He is within each human heart patiently awaiting our recognition that we are one with Him, that He is the goal of our life.

AUM—AMIN—AMEN

THE END

The film made during the course of our travels in India and Europe is entitled "The Lost Years." It has been syndicated to world-wide television and is available for rental, and sale on film, and video. For information write to:

Aura Productions
P.O. Box 46026
Los Angeles, CA 90046

Appendix

THE LIFE OF SAINT ISSA
"Best of the Sons of Men"

I.

1. The earth trembled and the heavens wept, because of the great crime committed in the land of Israel.

2. For there was tortured and murdered the great and just Issa, in whom was manifest the soul of the Universe;

3. Which had incarnated in a simple mortal, to benefit men and destroy the evil spirit in them;

4. To lead back to peace, love and happiness, man, degraded by his sins, and recall him to the one and indivisible Creator whose mercy is infinite.

5. The merchants coming from Israel have given the following account of what has occurred:

II.

1. The people of Israel—who inhabit a fertile country producing two harvests a year and affording pasture for large herds of cattle—by their sin brought down upon themselves the anger of the Lord;

2. Who inflicted upon them terrible chastisements, taking from them their land; their cattle and their wealth. They were carried away into slavery by the rich and mighty Pharaohs who then ruled the land of Egypt.

3. The Israelites were, by the Pharaohs, treated worse than beasts, condemned to hard labor and put in irons, their bodies were covered with wounds and sores; they were not permitted to live under a roof, and were starved to death;

4. That they might be maintained in a state of continual terror and deprived of all human resemblance;

5. And in this great calamity, the Israelites, remembering their Celestial Protector, implored his forgiveness and mercy.

6. At that period reigned in Egypt an illustrious Pharaoh, who was renowned for his many victories, immense riches, and the gigantic palaces he had erected by the labor of his slaves.

7. This Pharaoh had two sons, the younger of whom, named Mossa, had acquired much knowledge from the sages of Israel.

8. And Mossa was beloved by all in Egypt for his kindness of heart and the pity he showed to all sufferers.

9. When Mossa saw that the Israelites, in spite of their many sufferings, had not forsaken their God, and refused to worship the gods of Egypt, created by the hands of man.

10. He also put his faith in their invisible God, who did not suffer them to betray Him, despite their ever growing weakness.

11. And the teachers among Israel animated Mossa in his zeal, and prayed of him that he would intercede with his father, Pharaoh, in favor of their co-religionists.

12. Prince Mossa went before his father, begging him to lighten the burden of the unhappy people; Pharaoh, however, became incensed with rage, and ordered that they should be tormented more than before.

13. And it came to pass that Egypt was visited by a great calamity. The plague decimated young and old, the healthy and the sick; and Pharaoh beheld in this the resentment of his own gods against him.

14. But Prince Mossa said to his father that it was the God of his slaves who thus interposed on behalf of his wretched people, and avenged them upon the Egyptians.

15. Thereupon, Pharaoh commanded Mossa, his son, to gather all the Israelite slaves, and lead them away, and found, at a great distance from the capitol, another city where he should rule over them.

16. Then Mossa made known to the Hebrew slaves that he had obtained their freedom in the name of his and their God, the God of Israel; and with them he left the city and departed from the land of Egypt.

17. He led them back to the land which, because of their many sins, had been taken from them. There he gave them laws and admonished them to pray always to God, the indivisible Creator, whose kindness is infinite.

18. *After Prince Mossa's death, the Israelites observed rigorously his laws; and God rewarded them for the ills to which they had been subjected in Egypt.*

19. *Their kingdom became one of the most powerful on earth; their kings made themselves renowned for their treasures, and peace reigned in Israel.*

III.

1. *The glory of Israel's wealth spread over the whole earth, and the surrounding nations became envious.*

2. *But the Most High himself led the victorious arms of the Hebrews, and the Pagans did not dare to attack them.*

3. *Unfortunately, man is prone to err, and the fidelity of the Israelites to their God was not of long duration.*

4. *Little by little they forgot the favors he had bestowed upon them; rarely invoked his name, and sought protection by the magicians and sorcerers.*

5. *The kings and the chiefs among the people substituted their own laws for those given by Mossa; the temple of God and the observances of their ancient faith were neglected; the people addicted themselves to sensual gratifications and lost their original purity.*

6. *Many centuries had elapsed since their exodus from Egypt, when God bethought himself of again inflicting chastisement upon them.*

7. *Strangers invaded Israel, devastated the land, destroyed the villages, and carried their inhabitants away into captivity.*

8. *At last came the Pagans from over the sea, from the land of Romeles. These made themselves masters of the Hebrews, and placed over them their army chiefs, who governed in the name of Caesar.*

9. *They defiled the temples, forced the inhabitants to cease the worship of the indivisible God, and compelled them to sacrifice to the heathen gods.*

10. *They made common soldiers of those who had been men of rank; the women became their prey, and the common people, reduced to slavery, were carried away by thousands over the sea.*

11. *The children were slain, and soon, in the whole land, there was naught heard but weeping and lamentation.*

12. *In this extreme distress, the Israelites once more remembered their great God, implored his mercy and prayed for his forgiveness. Our Father, in his inexhaustible clemency, heard their prayer.*

IV.

1.   At that time the moment had come for the compassionate Judge to re-incarnate in a human form;

2.   And the eternal Spirit, resting in a state of complete inaction and supreme bliss, awakened and separated from the eternal Being, for an undetermined period,

3.   So that, in human form, He might teach man to identify himself with the Divinity and attain to eternal felicity;

4.   And to show, by His example, how man can attain moral purity and free his soul from the domination of the physical senses, so that it may achieve the perfection necessary for it to enter the Kingdom of Heaven, which is immutable and where bliss eternal reigns.

5.   Soon after, a marvellous child was born in the land of Israel. God himself spoke, through the mouth of this child, of the miseries of the body and the grandeur of the soul.

6.   The parents of the infant were poor people, who belonged to a family noted for great piety; who forgot the greatness of their ancestors in celebrating the name of the Creator and giving thanks to Him for the trials which He had sent upon them.

7.   To reward them for adhering to the path of truth, God blessed the first-born of this family; chose him for His elect, and sent him to sustain the fallen and comfort the afflicted.

8.   The divine child, to whom the name Issa was given, commenced in his tender years to talk of the only and indivisible God, exhorting the strayed souls to repent and purify themselves from the sins of which they had become guilty.

9.   People came from all parts to hear him, and marvelled at the discourses which came from his infantile mouth; and all Israel agreed that the Spirit of the Eternal dwelt in this child.

10.   When Issa was thirteen years old, the age at which the Israelite is expected to marry,

11.   The modest house of his industrious parents became a meeting-place of the rich and illustrious, who were anxious to have as a son-in-law the young Issa, who was already celebrated for the edifying discourses he made in the name of the All-Powerful.

12.   Then Issa secretly absented himself from his father's house; left Jerusalem, and, in a train of merchants, journeyed toward the Sindh,

13.   With the object of perfecting himself in the knowledge of the word of God and the study of the laws of the great Buddhas.

V.

1. In his fourteenth year, young Issa, the Blessed One, came this side of the Sindh and settled among the Aryas, in the country beloved by God.

2. Fame spread the name of the marvellous youth along the northern Sindh, and when he came through the country of the five streams and Radjipoutan, the devotees of the god Djaine asked him to stay among them.

3. But he left the deluded worshippers of Djaine and went to Djagguernat, in the country of Orsis, where repose the mortal remains of Vyassa-Krishna, and where the white priests of Brahma welcomed him joyfully.

4. They taught him to read and to understand the Vedas, to cure physical ills by means of prayer, to teach and to expound the sacred Scriptures, to drive out evil desires from man and make him again in the likeness of God.

5. He spent six years in Djagguernat, in Radjagriha, in Benares, and in other holy cities. The common people loved Issa, for he lived in peace with the Vaisyas and the Sudras, to whom he taught the Holy Scriptures.

6. But the Brahmins and the Kshatriyas told him that they were forbidden by the great Para-Brahma to come near to those who were created from his belly and his feet;*

7. That the Vaisyas might only hear the recital of the Vedas, and this only on the festival days, and

8. That the Sudras were not only forbidden to attend the reading of the Vedas, but even to look on them; for they were condemned to perpetual servitude, as slaves of the Brahmins, the Kshatriyas and even the Vaisyas.

9. "Death alone can enfranchise them from their servitude," has said Para-Brahma. "Leave them therefore, and come to adore with us the gods, whom you will make angry if you disobey them."

10. But Issa, disregarding their words, remained with the Sudras, preaching against the Brahmins and the Kshatriyas.

11. He declaimed strongly against man's arrogating to himself the authority to deprive his fellow-beings of their human and spiritual

---

*The Vaisyas and Sudras castes.

rights. "Verily," he said, "God has made no difference between his children, who are all alike dear to Him."

12. Issa denied the divine inspiration of the Vedas and the Puranas, for, as he taught his followers, "One law has been given to man to guide him in his actions:

13. "Fear the Lord, thy God; bend thy knees only before Him and bring to Him only the offerings which come from thy earnings."

14. Issa denied the Trimurti and the incarnation of Para-Brahma in Vishnu, Siva, and other gods; "for," said he:

15. "The eternal Judge, the eternal Spirit, constitutes the only and indivisible soul of the universe, and it is this soul alone which creates, contains and vivifies all.

16. "He alone has willed and created. He alone has existed from eternity, and His existence will be without end: there is no one like unto Him either in the heavens or on the earth.

17. "The great Creator has divided His power with no other being; far less with inanimate objects, as you have been taught to believe, for He alone is omnipotent and all-sufficient.

18. "He willed, and the world was. By one divine thought, He reunited the waters and separated them from the dry land of the globe. He is the cause of the mysterious life of man, into whom He has breathed part of His divine Being.

19. "And He has put under subjection to man, the lands, the waters, the beasts and everything which He created, and which He himself preserves in immutable order, alloting to each its proper duration.

20. "The anger of God will soon break forth upon man; for he has forgotten his Creator; he has filled His temples with abominations; and he adores a multitude of creatures which God has subordinated to him;

21. "And to gain favor with images of stone and metal, he sacrifices human beings in whom dwells part of the Spirit of the Most High;

22. "And he humiliates those who work in the sweat of their brows, to gain favor in the eyes of the idler who sitteth at a sumptuous table.

23. Those who deprive their brothers of divine happiness will themselves be deprived of it; and the Brahmins and the Kshatriyas shall become the Sudras of the Sudras, with whom the Eternal will stay forever.

24. "In the day of judgment the Sudras and the Vaisyas will be forgiven for they knew not the light, while God will let loose his wrath upon those who arrogated his authority."

25. The Vaisyas and the Sudras were filled with great admiration, and asked Issa how they should pray, in order not to lose their hold upon eternal life.

26. "Pray not to idols, for they cannot hear you; hearken not to the Vedas where the truth is altered; be humble and humiliate not your fellow-man.

27. "Help the poor, support the weak, do evil to none; covet not that which ye have not and which belongs to others."

VI.

1. The white priests and the warriors,* who had learned of Issa's discourse to the Sudras, resolved upon his death, and sent their servants to find the young teacher and slay him.

2. But Issa, warned by the Sudras of his danger, left by night Djag-guernat, gained the mountain, and settled in the country of the Gautamides, where the great Buddha Sakya-Muni came to the world, among a people who worshipped the only and sublime Brahma.

3. When the just Issa had acquired the Pali language, he applied himself to the study of the sacred scrolls of the Sutras.

4. After six years of study, Issa, whom the Buddha had elected to spread his holy word, could perfectly expound the sacred scrolls.

5. He then left Nepaul and the Himalaya mountains, descended into the valley of Radjipoutan and directed his steps toward the West, everywhere preaching to the people the supreme perfection attainable by man;

6. And the good he must do to his fellow-men, which is the sure means of speedy union with the eternal Spirit. "He who has recovered his primitive purity," said Issa, "shall die with his transgressions forgiven and have the right to contemplate the majesty of God."

7. When the divine Issa traversed the territories of the Pagans, he taught that the adoration of visible gods was contrary to natural law.

8. "For to man," said he, "it has not been given to see the image of God, and it behooves him not to make for himself a multitude of divinities in the imagined likeness of the Eternal.

9. "Moreover, it is against human conscience to have less regard for the greatness of divine purity, than for animals or works of stone or metal made by the hands of man.

---

*Brahmins and Kshatriyas.

10. "The eternal Lawgiver is One; there are no other Gods than He: He has parted the world with none, nor had He any counsellor.

11. "Even as a father shows kindness toward his children, so will God judge men after death, in conformity with His merciful laws. He will never humiliate his child by casting his soul for chastisement into the body of a beast.

12. "The heavenly laws," said the Creator, through the mouth of Issa, "are opposed to the immolation of human sacrifices to a statue or an animal; for I, the God, have sacrificed to man all the animals and all that the world contains.

13. "Everything has been sacrificed to man, who is directly and intimately united to me, his Father; therefore, shall the man be severely judged and punished by my law, who causes the sacrifice of my children.

14. "Man is naught before the eternal Judge; as the animal is before man.

15. "Therefore, I say unto you, leave your idols and perform not ceremonies which separate you from your Father and bind you to the priests, from whom heaven has turned away.

16. "For it is they who have led you away from the true God, and by superstitions and cruelty perverted the spirit and made you blind to the knowledge of the truth."

VII.

1. The words of Issa spread among the Pagans, through whose country he passed, and the inhabitants abandoned their idols.

2. Seeing which, the priests demanded of him who thus glorified the name of the true God, that he should, in the presence of the people, prove the charges he made against them, and demonstrate the vanity of their idols.

3. And Issa answered them: "If your idols, or the animals you worship, really possess the supernatural powers you claim, let them strike me with a thunder-bolt before you!"

4. "Why dost not thou perform a miracle," replied the priests, "and let thy God confound ours, if He is greater than they?"

5. But Issa said: "The miracles of our God have been wrought from the first day when the universe was created; and are performed every day and every moment; whoso sees them not is deprived of one of the most beautiful gifts of life.

6. *"And it is not on inanimate objects of stone, metal or wood that He will let His anger fall, but on the men who worship them, and who, therefore, for their salvation, must destroy the idols they have made.*

7. *"Even as a stone and a grain of sand, which are naught before man, await patiently their use by Him.*

8. *"In like manner, man, who is naught before God, must await in resignation His pleasure for a manifestation of His favor.*

9. *"But woe to you! ye adversaries of men, if it is not the favor you await, but rather the wrath of the Most High; woe to you, if you demand that He attest His power by a miracle!*

10. *"For it is not the idols which He will destroy in His wrath, but those by whom they were created; their hearts will be the prey of an eternal fire and their flesh shall be given to the beasts of prey.*

11. *"God will drive away the contaminated animals from His flocks; but will take to Himself those who strayed because they knew not the heavenly part within them."*

12. *When the Pagans saw that the power of their priests was naught, they put faith in the words of Issa. Fearing the anger of the true God, they broke their idols to pieces and caused their priests to flee from among them.*

13. *Issa furthermore taught the Pagans that they should not endeavor to see the eternal Spirit with their eyes; but to perceive Him with their hearts, and make themselves worthy of His favors by the purity of their souls.*

14. *"Not only,"* he said to them, *"must ye refrain from offering human sacrifices, but ye may not lay on the altar any creature to which life has been given, for all things created are for man.*

15. *"Withhold not from your neighbor his just due, for this would be like stealing from him what he had earned in the sweat of his brow.*

16. *"Deceive none, that ye may not yourselves be deceived; seek to justify yourselves before the last judgment, for then it will be too late.*

17. *"Be not given to debauchery, for it is a violation of the law of God.*

18. *"That you may attain to supreme bliss ye must not only purify yourselves, but must also guide others into the path that will enable them to regain their primitive innocence."*

VIII.

1. *The countries round about were filled with the renown of Issa's preachings, and when he came into Persia, the priests grew afraid and forbade the people hearing him;*

2.   *Nevertheless, the villagers received him with joy, and the people hearkened intently to his words, which, being seen by priests, caused them to order that he should be arrested and brought before their High Priest, who asked him:*

3.   *"Of what new God dost thou speak? Knowest thou not, unfortunate man that thou art! that Saint Zoroaster is the only Just One, to whom alone was vouchsafed the honor of receiving revelations from the Most High:*

4.   *"By whose command the angels compiled His Words in laws for the governance of His people, which were given to Zoroaster in Paradise?*

5.   *"Who, then, art thou, who darest to utter blasphemies against our God and sow doubts in the hearts of believers?"*

6.   *And Issa said to them: "I preach no new God, but our celestial Father, who has existed before the beginning and will exist until after the end.*

7.   *"Of Him I have spoken to the people, who—even as innocent children—are incapable of comprehending God by their own intelligence or fathoming the sublimity of the divine Spirit;*

8.   *"But, as the new-born child in the night recognizes the mother's breast, so your people, held in the darkness of error by your pernicious doctrines and religious ceremonies, have recognized instinctively their Father, in the Father whose prophet I am.*

9.   *"The eternal Being says to your people, by my mouth, 'Ye shall not adore the sun, for it is but a part of the universe which I have created for man;*

10.   *"It rises to warm you during your work; it sets to accord you the rest that I have ordained.*

11.   *"To me only ye owe all that ye possess, all that surrounds you and that is above and below you."*

12.   *"But," said the priests, "how could the people live according to your rules if they had no teachers?"*

13.   *Whereupon Issa answered: "So long as they had no priests, they were governed by the natural law and conserved the simplicity of their souls;*

14.   *"Their souls were in God and to commune with the Father they had not to have recourse to the intermediation of idols, or animals, or fire, as taught by you.*

15.   *"Ye pretend that man must adore the sun, and the Genii of Good and Evil. But I say unto you that your doctrine is pernicious. The sun*

*does not act spontaneously, but by the will of the invisible Creator,
who has given to it being."*

*16. "Who, then, has caused that this star lights the day, warms man at
his work and vivifies the seeds sown in the ground?"*

*17. "The eternal Spirit is the soul of everything animate, and you
commit a great sin in dividing Him into the Spirit of Evil and the Spirit
of Good, for there is no God other than the God of Good.*

*18. "And He, like to the father of a family, does only good to His
children, to whom He forgives their transgressions if they repent of
them.*

*19. "And the Spirit of Evil dwells upon earth, in the hearts of those
who turn the children of God away from the right path.*

*20. "Therefore, I say unto you: Fear the day of judgment, for God
will inflict a terrible chastisement upon all those who have led His
children astray and beguiled them with superstitions and errors;*

*21. "Upon those who have blinded them who saw; who have brought
contagion to the well; who have taught the worship of those things
which God made to be subject to man, or to aid him in his works.*

*22. "Your doctrine is the fruit of your error in seeking to bring near to
you the God of Truth, by creating for yourselves false gods."*

*23. When the Magi heard these words, they feared to themselves to do
him harm, but at night, when the whole city slept, they brought him
outside the walls and left him on the highway, in the hope that he
would not fail to become prey of wild beasts.*

*24. But, protected by the Lord our God, Saint Issa continued on his
way, without accident.*

IX.

*1. Issa—whom the Creator had selected to recall to the worship of the
true God, men sunk in sin—was twenty-nine years old when he arrived
in the land of Israel.*

*2. Since the departure therefrom of Issa, the Pagans had caused the
Israelites to endure more atrocious sufferings than before, and they
were filled with despair.*

*3. Many among them had begun to neglect the laws of their God, and
those of Mossa, in the hope of winning the favor of their brutal
conquerors.*

*4. But Issa, notwithstanding their unhappy condition, exhorted his
countrymen not to despair, because the day of their redemption from*

the yoke of sin was near, and he himself by his example, confirmed their faith in the God of their fathers.

5. "Children, yield not yourselves to despair," said the celestial Father to them, through the mouth of Issa, "for I have heard your lamentations, and your cries have reached my ears.

6. "Weep not, oh, my beloved sons! for your griefs have touched the heart of your Father and He has forgiven you, as He forgave your ancestors.

7. "Forsake not your families to plunge into debauchery; stain not the nobility of your souls; adore not idols which cannot but remain deaf to your supplications.

8. "Fill my temple with your hope and your patience, and do not adjure the religion of your forefathers, for I have guided them and bestowed upon them my beneficence.

9. "Lift up those who are fallen; feed the hungry and help the sick, that ye may be altogether pure and just in the day of the last judgment which I prepare for you."

10. The Israelites came in multitudes to listen to Issa's words, and they asked him where they should thank their Heavenly Father, since their enemies had demolished their temples and robbed them of their sacred vessels.

11. Issa told them that God cared not for temples erected by human hands, but that human hearts were the true temples of God.

12. "Enter into your temple, into your heart; illuminate it with good thoughts, with patience and the unshakeable faith which you owe to your Father.

13. "And your sacred vessels! they are your hands and your eyes. Look to do that which is agreeable to God, for in doing good to your fellow-men, you perform a ceremony that embellishes the temple wherein abideth Him who has created you.

14. "For God has created you in His own image, innocent, with pure souls, and hearts filled with kindness and not made for the planning of evil, but to be the sanctuaries of love and justice.

15. "Therefore, I say unto you, soil not your hearts with evil, for in them the Eternal Being abides.

16. "When ye do works of devotion and love, let them be with full hearts, and see that the motives of your actions be not hopes of gain or self-interest;

17. "For actions, so impelled, will not bring you nearer to salvation,

but lead to a state of moral degradation wherein theft, lying and murder pass for generous deeds."

X.

1. Issa went from one city to another, strengthening by the word of God the courage of the Israelites, who were near to succumbing under their weight of woe, and thousands of people followed him to hear his teachings.

2. But the chiefs of the cities were afraid of him and they informed the principal governor, residing in Jerusalem, that a man called Issa had arrived in the country, who by his sermons had arrayed the people against the authorities, and that multitudes listening assiduously to him, neglected their labor; and they added, he said that in a short time they would be free of their invader rulers.

3. Then Pilate, the Governor of Jerusalem, gave orders that they should lay hold of the preacher Issa and bring him before the judges. In order, however, not to excite the anger of the populace, Pilate directed that he should be judged by the priests and scribes, the Hebrew elders, in their temple.

4. Meanwhile, Issa, continuing his preachings, arrived at Jerusalem, and the people, who already knew his fame, having learned of his coming, went out to meet him.

5. They greeted him respectfully and opened to him the doors of their temple, to hear from his mouth what he had said in other cities of Israel.

6. And Issa said to them: "The human race perishes, because of the lack of faith; for the darkness and the tempest have caused the flock to go astray and they have lost their shepherds.

7. "But the tempests do not rage forever and the darkness will not hide the light eternally; soon the sky will become serene, the celestial light will again overspread the earth, and the strayed flock will re-unite around their shepherd.

8. "Wander not in the darkness, seeking the way, lest ye fall into the ditch; but gather together, sustain one another, put your faith in God and wait for the first glimmer of light to re-appear.

9. He who sustains his neighbor, sustains himself; and he who protects his family, protects all his people and his country.

10. "For, be assured that the day is near when you will be delivered from the darkness; you will be re-united into one family and your

enemy will tremble with fear, he who is ignorant of the favor of the great God."

11. The priests and the elders who heard him, filled with admiration for his language, asked him if it was true that he had sought to raise the people against the authorities of the country, as had been reported to the governor Pilate.

12. "Can one raise against estrayed men, to whom darkness has hidden their road and their door?" answered Issa. "I have but forewarned the unhappy, as I do here in this temple, that they should no longer advance on the dark road, for an abyss opens before their feet.

13. "The power of this earth is not of long duration and is subject to numberless changes. It would be of no avail for a man to rise in revolution against it, for one phase of it always succeeds another, and it is thus that it will go on until the extinction of human life.

14. "But do you not see that the powerful, and the rich, sow among the children of Israel a spirit of rebellion against the eternal power of Heaven?"

15. Then the elders asked him: "Who art thou, and from what country hast thou come to us? We have not formerly heard thee spoken of and do not even know thy name!"

16. "I am an Israelite," answered Issa; "and on the day of my birth have seen the walls of Jerusalem, and have heard the sobs of my brothers reduced to slavery, and the lamentations of my sisters carried away by the Pagans;

18. "But, having heard it said that my brethren suffered even greater miseries now, I have come back to the land of my fathers, to recall my brethren to the faith of their ancestors, which teaches us patience upon earth in order to attain the perfect and supreme bliss above."

19. Then the wise old men put to him again this question: "We are told that thou disownest the laws of Mossa, and that thou teachest the people to forsake the temple of God?"

20. Whereupon Issa: "One does not demolish that which has been given by our Heavenly Father, and which has been destroyed by sinners. I have but enjoined the people to purify the heart of all stains, for it is the veritable temple of God.

21. "As regards the laws of Mossa, I have endeavored to re-establish them in the hearts of men; and I say unto you that ye ignore their true meaning, for it is not vengeance but pardon which they teach. Their sense has been perverted."

XI.

1.   When the priests and the elders heard Issa, they decided among themselves not to give judgment against him, for he had done no harm to any one, and, presenting themselves before Pilate—who was made Governor of Jerusalem by the Pagan king of the country of Romeles— they spake to him thus:

2.   "We have seen the man whom thou chargest with inciting our people to revolt; we have heard his discourses and know that he is our countryman;

3.   "But the chiefs of the cities have made to you false reports, for he is a just man, who teaches the people the word of God. After interrogating him, we have allowed him to go in peace."

4.   The governor thereupon became very angry, and sent his disguised spies to keep watch upon Issa and report to the authorities the least word he addressed to the people.

5.   In the meantime, the holy Issa continued to visit the neighboring cities and preach the true way of the Lord, enjoining the Hebrews patience and promising them speedy delivery.

6.   And all the time great numbers of the people followed him wherever he went, and many did not leave him at all, but attached themselves to him and served him.

7.   And Issa said: "Put not your faith in miracles performed by the hands of men, for He who rules nature is alone capable of doing supernatural things, while man is impotent to arrest the wrath of the winds, or cause the rain to fall.

8.   "One miracle, however, is within the power of man to accomplish. It is, when his heart is filled with sincere faith, he resolves to root out from his mind all evil promptings and desires, and when, in order to attain this end, he ceases to walk the path of iniquity.

9.   "All the things done without God are only gross errors, illusions and seductions, serving but to show how much the heart of the doer is full of presumption, falsehood and impurity.

10.   "Put not your faith in oracles. God alone knows the future. He who has recourse to the diviners soils the temple of his heart and shows his lack of faith in his Creator.

11.   "Belief in the diviners and their miracles destroys the innate simplicity of man and his childlike purity. An infernal power takes hold of him who so errs, and forces him to commit various sins and give himself to the worship of idols.

12. "But the Lord our God, to whom none can be equalled, is one omnipotent, omniscient and omnipresent; He alone possesses all wisdom and all light.

13. "To Him ye must address yourselves, to be comforted in your afflictions, aided in your works, healed in your sickness and whoso asks of Him, shall not ask in vain.

14. "The secrets of nature are in the hands of God, for the whole world, before it was made manifest, existed in the bosom of the divine thought, and has become material and visible by the will of the Most High.

15. "When ye pray to him, become again like little children, for ye know neither the past, nor the present, nor the future, and God is the Lord of Time."

XII.

1. "Just man," said to him the disguised spies of the Governor of Jerusalem, "tell us if we must continue to do the will of Caesar, or expect our near deliverance?"

2. And Issa, who recognized the questioners as the apostate spies sent to follow him, replied to them: "I have not told you that you would be delivered from Caesar; it is the soul sunk in error which will gain its deliverance.

3. "There cannot be a family without a head, and there cannot be order in a people without a Caesar, whom ye should implicitly obey, as he will be held to answer for his acts before the Supreme Tribunal."

4. "Does Caesar possess a divine right?" the spies asked him again; "and is he the best of mortals?"

5. "There is no one 'the best' among human beings; but there are many bad, who—even as the sick need physicians—require the care of those chosen for that mission, in which must be used the means given by the sacred law of our Heavenly Father;

6. "Mercy and justice are the high prerogatives of Caesar, and his name will be illustrious if he exercises them.

7. "But he who acts otherwise, who transcends the limits of power he has over those under his rule, and even goes so far as to put their lives in danger, offends the great Judge and derogates from his own dignity in the eyes of men."

8. Upon this, an old woman who had approached the group, to better hear Issa, was pushed aside by one of the disguised men, who placed himself before her.

9. Then said Issa: "It is not good for a son to push away his mother, that he may occupy the place which belongs to her. Whoso doth not respect his mother—the most sacred being after his God—is unworthy of the name of son.

10. "Hearken to what I say to you: Respect woman; for in her we see the mother of the universe, and all the truth of divine creation is to come through her.

11. "She is the fount of everything good and beautiful, as she is also the germ of life and death. Upon her man depends in all his existence, for she is his moral and natural support in his labors.

12. "In pain and suffering she brings you forth; in the sweat of her brow she watches over your growth, and until her death you cause her greatest anxieties. Bless her and adore her, for she is your only friend and support on earth.

13. "Respect her; defend her. In so doing you will gain for yourself her love; you will find favor before God, and for her sake many sins will be remitted to you.

14. "Love your wives and respect them, for they will be the mothers of tomorrow and later the grandmothers of a whole nation.

15. "Be submissive to the wife; her love ennobles man, softens his hardened heart, tames the wild beast in him and changes it to a lamb.

16. "Wife and mother are the priceless treasures which God has given to you. They are the most beautiful ornaments of the universe, and from them will be born all who will inhabit the world.

17. "Even as the Lord of Hosts separated the light from the darkness, and the dry land from the waters, so does woman possess the divine gift calling forth out of man's evil nature all the good that is in him.

18. "Therefore I say unto you, after God, to woman must belong your best thoughts, for she is the divine temple where you will most easily obtain perfect happiness.

19. "Draw from this temple your moral force. There you will forget your sorrows and your failures, and recover the love necessary to aid your fellow-men.

20. "Suffer her not to be humiliated, for by humiliating her you humiliate yourselves, and lose the sentiment of love, without which nothing can exist here on earth.

21. "Protect your wife, that she may protect you—you and all your household. All that you do for your mothers, your wives, for a widow, or for any other woman in distress, you will do for your God."

XIII.

1.   Thus Saint Issa taught the people of Israel for three years, in every city and every village, on the highways and in the fields, and all he said came to pass.

2.   All this time the disguised spies of the governor Pilate observed him closely, but heard nothing to sustain the accusations formerly made against Issa by the chiefs of the cities.

3.   But Saint Issa's growing popularity did not allow Pilate to rest. He feared that Issa would be instrumental in bringing about a revolution culminating in his elevation to the sovereignty, and, therefore, ordered the spies to make charges against him.

4.   Then soldiers were sent to arrest him, and they cast him into a subterranean dungeon, where he was subjected to all kinds of tortures, to compel him to accuse himself, so that he might be put to death.

5.   The Saint, thinking only of the perfect bliss of his brethren, endured all those torments with resignation to the will of the Creator.

6.   The servants of Pilate continued to torture him, and he was reduced to a state of extreme weakness; but God was with him and did not permit him to die at their hands.

7.   When the principal priests and wise elders learned of the sufferings which their Saint endured, they went to Pilate, begging him to liberate Issa, so that he might attend the great festival which was near at hand.

8.   But this the governor refused. Then they asked him that Issa should be brought before the elders' council, so that he might be condemned, or acquitted, before the festival, and to this Pilate agreed.

9.   On the following day the governor assembled the principal chiefs, priests, elders and judges, for the purpose of judging Issa.

10. The Saint was brought from his prison. They made him sit before the governor, between two robbers, who were to be judged at the same time with Issa, so as to show the people he was not the only one to be condemned.

11. And Pilate, addressing himself to Issa said, "Is it true, Oh! Man; that thou incitest the populace against the authorities, with the purpose of thyself becoming King of Israel?"

12. Issa replied, "One does not become king by one's own purpose thereto. They have told you an untruth when you were informed that I was inciting the people to revolution. I have only preached of the King of Heaven, and it was Him whom I told the people to worship.

13. "For the sons of Israel have lost their original innocence and unless

224

they return to worship the true God they will be sacrificed and their temple will fall in ruins.

14. "The worldly power upholds order in the land; I told them not to forget this. I said to them, 'Live in conformity with your situation and refrain from disturbing public order; and, at the same time, I exhorted them to remember that disorder reigned in their own hearts and spirits.

15. "Therefore, the King of Heaven has punished them, and has destroyed their nationality and taken from them their national kings, 'but,' I added, 'if you will be resigned to your fate, as a reward the Kingdom of Heaven will be yours."

16. At this moment the witnesses were introduced; one of whom deposed thus: "Thou has said to the people that in comparison with the power of the king who would soon liberate the Israelites from the yoke of the heathen, the worldly authorities amounted to nothing."

17. "Blessings upon thee!" said Issa. "For thou hast spoken the truth! The King of Heaven is greater and more powerful than the laws of man and His kingdom surpasses the kingdoms of this earth.

18. "And the time is not far off, when Israel, obedient to the will of God, will throw off its yoke of sin, for it has been written that a forerunner would appear to announce the deliverance of the people, and that he would re-unite them in one family."

19. Thereupon the governor said to the judges: "Have you heard this? The Israelite Issa acknowledges the crime of which he is accused. Judge him, then, according to your laws and pass upon him condemnation to death."

20. "We cannot condemn him," replied the priests and the ancients. "As thou hast heard, he spoke of the King of Heaven, and he has preached nothing which constitutes insubordination against the law."

21. Thereupon the governor called a witness who had been bribed by his master, Pilate, to betray Issa, and this man said to Issa: "Is it not true that thou has represented thyself as a King of Israel, when thou didst say that He who reigns in Heaven sent thee to prepare His people?"

22. But Issa blessed the man and answered: "Thou wilt find mercy, for what thou hast said did not come out from thine own heart." Then, turning to the governor he said: "Why dost thou lower thy dignity and teach thy inferiors to tell falsehood, when, without doing so, it is in thy power to condemn an innocent man?"

23. When Pilate heard his words, he became greatly enraged and

ordered that Issa be condemned to death, and that the two robbers should be declared guiltless.

24. The judges, after consulting among themselves, said to Pilate: "We cannot consent to take this great sin upon us—to condemn an innocent man and liberate malefactors. It would be against our laws.

25. "Act thyself, then, as thou seest fit." Thereupon the priests and elders walked out, and washed their hands in a sacred vessel, and said: "We are innocent of the blood of this righteous man."

XIV.

1. By order of the governor, the soldiers seized Issa and the two robbers, and led them to the place of execution, where they were nailed upon the crosses erected for them.

2. All day long the bodies of Issa and the two robbers hung upon the crosses, bleeding, guarded by the soldiers. The people stood all around and the relatives of the executed prayed and wept.

3. When the sun went down, Issa's tortures ended. He lost consciousness and his soul disengaged itself from the body, to reunite with God.

4. Thus ended the terrestrial existence of the reflection of the eternal Spirit under the form of a man who had saved hardened sinners and comforted the afflicted.

5. Meanwhile, Pilate was afraid for what he had done, and ordered the body of the Saint to be given to his relatives, who put it in a tomb near to the place of execution. Great numbers of persons came to visit the tomb, and the air was filled with their wailings and lamentations.

6. Three days later, the governor sent his soldiers to remove Issa's body and bury it in some other place, for he feared a rebellion among the people.

7. The next day, when the people came to the tomb, they found it open and empty, the body of Issa being gone. Thereupon, the rumor spread that the Supreme Judge had sent His angels from Heaven, to remove the mortal remains of the saint in whom part of the divine Spirit had lived on earth.

8. When Pilate learned of this rumor, he grew angry and prohibited, under penalty of death, the naming of Issa, or praying for him to the Lord.

9. But the people, nevertheless, continued to weep over Issa's death and to glorify their master, wherefore, many were carried into captivity, subjected to torture and put to death.

10. And the disciples of Saint Issa departed from the land of Israel and went in all directions, to the heathen, preaching that they should abandon their gross errors, think of the salvation of their souls and earn the perfect bliss which awaits human beings in the immaterial world, full of glory, where the great Creator abides in all his immaculate and perfect majesty.

11. The heathen, their kings, and their warriors, listened to the preachers, abandoned their erroneous beliefs and forsook their priests and their idols, to celebrate the praises of the most wise Creator of the Universe, the King of Kings, whose heart is filled with infinite mercy.

NOTES

Chapter 1
1. Durant, Caesar and Christ, p. 558.

Chapter 3
1. Luke 2:49.
2. Luke 2:46.
3. Notovitch, The Legend of Saint Issa, Chap. IV, V:10-13.
4. Durant, Caesar and Christ, p. 537.
5. Matthew 13:54.

Chapter 5
1. Notovitch, The Legend of Saint Issa, Chap. IV, V:12.
2. Ibid., V:12.
3. Das, Bhagavan, The Essential Unity of All Religions, p. XXX.
4. Exodus, 29.
5. Luke 2:22-24.

Chapter 6
1. Notovitch, The Legend of Saint Issa, V:3.
2. Ibid., V:5.
3. Vivekananda, The Yogas and Other Works.

Chapter 7
1. Notovitch, The Legend of Saint Issa, V:5.

Chapter 9
1. Notovitch, The Legend of Saint Issa, IV:10-13.
2. Ibid., XII:10-21.

Chapter 11
1. Notovitch, The Legend of Saint Issa, V:13.
2. Ibid., V:13.
3. Ibid., V:13-18.
4. Ibid., V:23-24.
5. Ibid., VI:1.
6. Ibid., VI:2.
7. Schulberg, L., Historic India, p. 79.
8. Ibid., p. 80.
9.

Chapter 13
1. John 20:24-29.
2. Matthew 28:16-20.
3. D'Souza, Rev. H., In the Steps of St. Thomas, p. 5.
4. Ibid., p. 5.
5. Ibid., p. 7.
6. Ibid., p. 7.
7. Ibid., p. 57.
8. Ibid., p. 61.
9. Ibid., p. 37.

NOTES

Chapter 14
1. Notovitch, The Legend of Saint Issa, IV:1.
2. John 1:24-34.
3. Luke 1:36.
4. Dimont, M., Jews, God and History, p. 135.

Chapter 15
1. Head, J. and Cranston, S. L., Ed., Reincarnation: The Phoenix Fire Mystery, p. 134.
2. Cambridge Medieval History, I, 121.
3. Encyclopaedia Brittanica, 11th Edition, Vol. 19, p. 641.
4. Read, A., Edgar Cayce on Jesus and His Church, p. 12.
5. Furst, J., Edgar Cayce's Story of Jesus.
6. Read, A., Edgar Cayce on Jesus and His Church, p. 13.
7. Ibid., p. 14.
8. Yogananda, Paramahansa, Man's Eternal Quest, p. 306.
9. Proverbs 8:22.
10. Matthew 17:9-13.
11. Luke 9:7, 8.
12. John 8:56-59.
13. Matthew 11:10.
14. John 1:14, 15.
15. Matthew 5:18.
16. Ibid., 5:21, 22.
17. Ibid., 5:14.
18. Ibid., 7:1, 2.
19. Ibid., 7:12.
20. Mark 2:5.
21. Read, A., Edgar Cayce on Jesus and His Church, p. 14.
22. John 10:30.

Chapter 16
1. Notovitch, The Legend of Saint Issa, V:4.
2. John 4:48.
3. American Heritage Dictionary of the English Language.
4. Emerson, Ralph Waldo, Compensation.
5. John 10:30.
6. Luke 8:45-48.
7. The Gospel of Sri Ramakrishna, p. 245.
8. Luke 23:50 through 24:3.
9. Bulst, Werner, The Shroud of Turin, p. 22.
10. Wilcox, R., The Shroud.
11. Ibid.

Chapter 17
1. Bhagavan Sri Sathya Sai Baba, Sathya Sai Baba Speaks, Vol. VI, No. 48.
2. Bhagavan Sri Sathya Sai Baba, Sanathana Sarathi, Jan., 1978.

Chapter 18
1. Satprakashananda, Swami, Hinduism and Christianity, p. 28.
2. John 1;1.
3. Das, Bhagavan, The Essential Unity of All Religions, p. 298.
4. Ibid., p. 298.

NOTES

5. Ibid., p. 298.
6. Ibid., p. 298.
7. Ibid., p. 298.
8. Satprakashananda, Swami, Hinduism and Christianity, p. 101.
9. Ibid., p. 101.
10. Ibid., p. 25.
11. John 6:35.
12. Satprakashananda, Swami, Hinduism and Christianity, p. 133.
13. Ibid., p. 95.
14. Luke 17:20, 21.
15. Matthew 13:33.
16. Satprakashananda, Swami, Hinduism and Christianity, p. 23.
17. Ibid., p. 23.
18. Ibid., p. 23.
19. Paramananda, Christ and Oriental Ideals, p. 135.
20. Ibid., p. 135.
21. Ibid., p. 135.
22. Ibid., p. 127.
23. Ibid., p. 126.
24. Ibid., p. 127.
25. Ibid., p. 128.
26. Ibid., p. 129.
27. Ibid., p. 126.
28. Satprakashananda, Swami, Hinduism and Christianity, p. 35.
29. John 8:42.
30. Das, Bhagavan, The Essential Unity of All Religions, p. 310.
31. Ibid., p. 310.
32. Ibid., p. 311.
33. Ibid., p. 311.
34. Ibid., p. 312.
35. Ibid., p. 300.
36. Ibid., p. 308.
37. Ibid., p. 309.
38. Ibid., p. 309.
39. Ibid., p. 308.
40. Ibid., p. 426.
41. Ibid., p. 436.
42. Ibid., p. 430.
43. Ibid., p. 429.
44. Ibid., p. 429.
45. Ibid., p. 60.
46. Ibid., p. 61.
47. Ibid., p. 61.
48. Ibid., p. 61.
49. Ibid., p. 61.
50. Ibid., p. 62.
51. Ibid., p. 62.

BIBLIOGRAPHY

Abhedananda, Swami, The Great Saviours of the World, Calcutta, 1947.

Abhedananda, Swami, Kashmiri O Tibetti (Bengali), Calcutta,

Bulst, S. J., The Shroud of Turin, Milwaukee, 1956.

Collins, L. and LaPierre, D., Freedom at Midnight, New York, 1975.

Das, Bhagavan, The Essential Unity of All Religions, London, 1973.

Dimont, Max I., Jews, God and History, New York, 1962.

D'Souza, Rev. Herman, In The Steps of St. Thomas, Madras, 1972.

Durant, Will, Caesar and Christ, New York, 1944.

Furst, J., Edgar Cayce's Story of Jesus, New York, 1968.

Head, J., and Cranston, S. L. (ed.), Reincarnation: The Phoenix Fire Mystery, New York, 1977.

Murphet, Howard, Man of Miracles, London, 1971.

Notovitch, Nicolas, The Unknown Life of Jesus Christ, New York, 1890.

Paramananda, Swami, Christ and Oriental Ideals, Cohasset, Mass., 1968.

Potter, Rev. Dr. C. F., The Lost Years of Jesus Revealed, Greenwich, Conn., 1962.

Read, Anne, Edgar Cayce on Jesus and His Church, New York, 1970.

Satprakashananda, Swami, Hinduism and Christianity, St. Louis, 1975.

Schulberg, L., Historic India, New York, 1968.

Vivekananda, Swami, The Yogas and Other Works, New York, 1953.

Wilcox, Robert, The Shroud, New York, 1975.

Yogananda, Paramahansa, Autobiography of a Yogi, Los Angeles, 1946.

Yogananda, Paramahansa, Man's Eternal Quest, Los Angeles, 1975.

Yukteswar, Swami, The Holy Science, Los Angeles, 1972.